RUGBY LEAGUE
The Skills of the Game

RUGBY LEAGUE

The Skills of the Game

MAURICE BAMFORD

THE CROWOOD PRESS

First published in 1989 by
The Crowood Press
Ramsbury, Marlborough
Wiltshire SN8 2HE

British Library Cataloguing in Publication Data

Bamford, Maurice
   Rugby League: the skills of the game.
   1. Rugby League football. Manuals
   I. Title
   796.33'32

   ISBN 1-85223-197-1

**Dedicated to Rita, my wife and friend — a true Rugby League
'grass' widow**

Acknowledgements
I am grateful to Phil Larder, Director of Coaching, and all in the
Rugby League National Coaching Scheme for years of enjoyment;
to Les Bettinson, Great Britain Team Manager, for guidance and
sound advice; to Andrew Varley of the Varley Picture Agency for
all his help and generosity in providing all photographs included in
the book; to Harry Edgar, editor of Open Rugby, for his support; to
Gary Schofield and his Leeds RLFC team mates for their
assistance; to Laurie Gant and Albert Fearnley for putting me on
the right path; and to Moira Smith for all her hours of hard work at
the typewriter.

Line illustrations by Ursula Matthews

Typeset by Action Typesetting Ltd, Gloucester
Printed in Great Britain by The Bath Press

Contents

1 The Team and its Coach 1
2 Developing the Basic Skills 7
3 Team Skills in Attack and Defence 76
4 The Kicking Game 104
5 Fitness and Nutrition 109
6 Football Psychology 116
7 Mini-League 118
  Glossary 120
  Index 121

Maurice Bamford has had playing and coaching involvement for over forty years in Rugby League football. Playing professional football for Hull FC and Dewsbury, he made the transition to coaching via the amateur game at Stanningley ARLFC. Other amateur coaching posts were held at the Milford, Oulton and Dudley Hill Junior Clubs, while his professional involvements have taken him to senior coaching appointments for Great Britain, Dewsbury (twice), Halifax, Huddersfield, Wigan, Bramley, Leeds (twice) and Workington Town. His full-time occupations have included Rugby League Development Officer for Leeds City Council, Commercial Manager for Leeds RLFC and Promotions Manager for Leeds United AFC.

Maurice Bamford has two loves in his life — his family and Rugby League. His 13-a-side courtship began as a schoolboy in the Rugby League community of Kirkstall in Leeds, maturing through every sector of the game to provide the vast experience on which the contents of this book are built. Maurice knows first hand the ups and downs of the rollercoaster world of Rugby League having been through it all — on and off the field — from the bottom to the very top.

Having risen through the amateur ranks as a player he entered the professional arena as a second-row forward with Dewsbury, Hull and Batley. He took the reins as coach of Dewsbury for a short spell in 1974, and first tasted success with Halifax at the end of the 1970s, guiding them from the depths of despair to Challenge Cup semi-final, Yorkshire Cup final and promotion glory. After a season with lowly Huddersfield, Maurice was elevated to coach of glamour-club Wigan for the 1981–2 season, then went back to the Second Division with Bramley before relaunching into the big time with Yorkshire's number one club Leeds, lifting the prestigious John Player Special Trophy.

Ultimate recognition came with his appointment as coach of Great Britain in the mid-1980s. Family loyalty forced his departure from the international scene at the end of 1986, Leeds immediately reappointing him to his Headingley role. Maurice is now charged with revitalising the fortunes of Dewsbury.

Maurice has also been a leading figure in the National Coaching Scheme, serving as a Regional Coach. He was the first ever Local Development Officer and has both coached amateur clubs and held administrative positions with professional clubs. His vast experience is combined with insight, vision and a deep passion for the 13-a-side code, as is evident in this welcome addition to Rugby League's ever-growing library.

David Howes
Rugby Football League Public Relations Officer

Maurice Bamford has the unique experience of having coached Rugby League at all levels, including the Great Britain team in series against France, New Zealand and Australia. In over forty years as a player and coach he has never lost his enthusiasm for the game and this is clearly displayed in *Rugby League*.

Maurice has always been a keen student of the game, prepared to experiment with new techniques and approaches. These ideas are now set out in such a way as to interest and appeal to readers of all ages who are keen to learn more about the skills and tactics of Rugby League. I thoroughly enjoyed reading *Rugby League* and am confident that you will also.

Les Bettinson
GB Rugby League Team Manager
President of the Rugby Football League

1 The Team and its Coach

THE TEAM

A Rugby League team consists of thirteen players plus two substitutes. The thirteen players comprise seven backs and six forwards, and the two substitutes are either two backs, two forwards or one of each. The positional name and required abilities for proficiency of each team member are as follows:

Team No.	Positional name	Required ability
1	Fullback	Speed, good defence, catching and kicking skills, awareness, strength, courage.
2	Right wing three-quarter	Speed, evasive skills, strength, good defence, courage.
3	Right centre three-quarter	Speed, handling skills, strength, good defence, game awareness, courage, evasive skills.
4	Left centre three-quarter	Speed, handling skills, strength, good defence, game awareness, courage, evasive skills.
5	Left wing three-quarter	Speed, evasive skills, strength, good defence, courage.
6	Stand-off half	Game awareness, handling skills, evasive skills, speed, courage, good defence, kicking skills.
7	Scrum half	Game awareness, handling skills, evasive skills, speed, courage, good defence, kicking skills.
8	Open-side prop forward	Strength, scrummaging technique, good defence, game awareness, stamina, handling skills, courage.
9	Hooker	Scrummaging technique, speed, flexibility, handling skills, strength, game awareness, good defence, stamina, courage.

10	Blind-side prop forward	Strength, scrummaging technique, good defence, game awareness, stamina, handling skills, courage.
11	Open-side second-row forward	Speed, strength, good defence, courage, stamina, handling skills, game awareness.
12	Blind-side second-row forward	Speed, strength, good defence, courage, stamina, handling skills, game awareness.
13	Loose forward	Speed, strength, good defence, courage, stamina, handling skills, game awareness, kicking skills.
14	Substitute	A utility three-quarter or general experienced 'back'.
15	Substitute	A utility forward with general experience in all positions from No.8 to No.13.

The game of Rugby League Football is a team game and great efforts should be made to encourage teamwork. The overall objects of the game are to score tries and kick goals. Which player scores the try or kicks the goal does not matter. Some teams rely on a gifted player to score individual tries or on a physically strong player to smash through smaller tacklers each time he is in possession of the football. But to be able to include individual match winners or naturally gifted players in your team is a very big bonus. It is far better to rely on smart teamwork, and far more enjoyable for all the team if the emphasis is placed on teamwork in training and in games.

Not only should combinations of play between team members be practised regularly in training, but a 'team spirit' should also be developed. A pride in the team's discipline and in the team's club, county, district or even country, a pride in each individual player and, above all, a pride in the game of Rugby League should be instilled in each and every young player.

Determination too — determination in attaining maximum fitness, learning the game, practising its skills and achieving the highest enjoyment from taking part. It is so much easier to enjoy any sporting competition when you are fit and skilful.

The answer to teamwork, or how to achieve it, is simple: practise the individual skills of the game and then channel those individual skills into team skills. Looking through our earlier list of required abilities, several of them are repeated over and over again. In fact all requirements can be broken down into two headings: coaching points and conditioning points. Handling, kicking, defensive and evasive skills, scrummaging techniques, game awareness and courage are coaching points; conditioning points include speed, stamina, strength and flexibility.

The general skills — handling, kicking, etc. — are self-explanatory, but game awareness and courage are perhaps less so. Game awareness is a state of mind; it means being able to 'read' a game. For

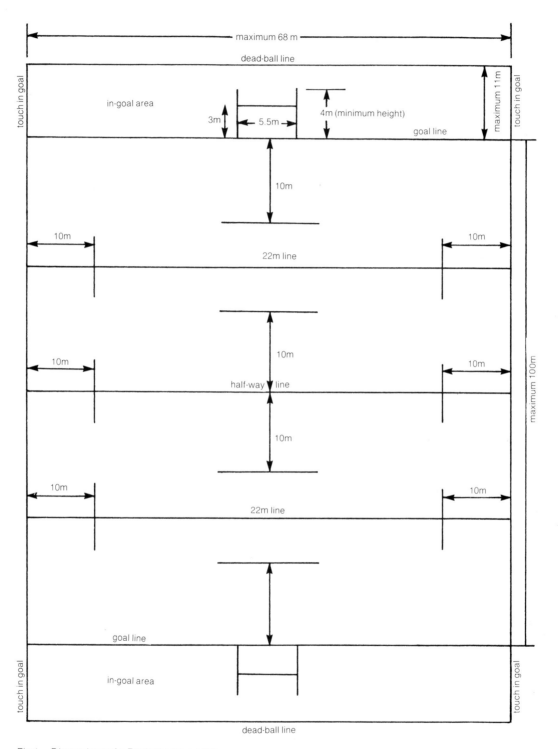

maximum 68 m

dead-ball line

touch in goal

in-goal area

3m

5.5m

4m (minimum height)

goal line

maximum 11m

touch in goal

10m

10m

10m

22m line

10m

10m

10m

10m

half-way line

maximum 100m

10m

10m

10m

22m line

10m

goal line

touch in goal

in-goal area

touch in goal

dead-ball line

Fig 1   Dimensions of a Rugby League pitch.

3

instance in support play, when a team mate bursts through the opposition's defence, the player with game awareness would already have weighed up the situation and would be in a position to support his team mate in the attack. In defence, a player possessing game awareness would 'fill in' a defensive hole in his team's line of defence, and so on.

Courage, too, is an essential requirement, and one developed through the player's own confidence. Good coaching, good advice and good skills practice help to build confidence and thus to produce a courageous player. The team needs all its players to be full of game awareness and courage. Add skills to these two factors and you have a team with all the abilities for success. We will return to the encouragement and development of these abilities in Chapter 2.

THE TEAM CAPTAIN

Most coaches select the team captain. This is an important selection, more important than selecting the whole team. The captain is an extension of the coach on the field of play. When selecting a captain the coach must look firstly for the quality of leadership. It is not always true that the best player makes the best captain. Being popular with his players is a good sign. But add to this enthusiasm, experience, consistency and a level head and you may have found your man.

A good coach—captain relationship is vital within a well organised team. The coach should take his captain into his confidence and should consider very carefully any changes the captain suggests for the good of the team. The clear-thinking coach will consult his captain on team selection and seek his advice on certain aspects of team welfare. The captain should also be spokesman for his team and fairly regular meetings should be held between coach and captain to discuss points made by the team that may need clarification.

Some experts consider that certain playing positions are ideal for a captain: a scrum half is near his forwards and links with his three-quarters; a fullback can see everything in front of him on both attack and defence; a centre or stand-off half has that extra time to assess the situation; a forward is in the thick of the action. Each position has its good and bad points. Look back through our game's history and think of the variety of positions that have successfully captained our country at international level — the late Clive Sullivan from the wing position, Frank Myler and Roger Millward from stand-off half, Alan Prescott from open-side prop, the grand old man of Rugby League Joe Egan from hooker and, in my international coaching days, Andy Goodway, second row, Ellery Hanley, centre and stand-off half, Harry Pinner from loose forward and David Watkinson from hooker.

So there is a good cross-section of positions for the captaincy. Which one fits the bill? It all depends on what your requirements are at the time, or what calibre of individual is available for your selection. One thing is for sure, your man must be in possession of the attributes necessary to ensure enjoyment and success on the field of play.

THE COACH

Most coaches are former players who have usually drifted into coaching because they are either too old to play or have had the back luck to receive an injury which curtails their playing career. Other coaches become involved in their chosen sport because of the participation of their son or daughter, niece or nephew or some other family connection. Whatever their motivation, all have one thing in common: responsibility for their pupil or team. The coach is responsible. The coach is decision maker. The coach is king. What makes a usually intelligent, nice, pleasant person decide to take on the responsibilities and pressures of the coach? What in fact makes a coach?

To start with, the old adage in our beloved game is 'Players win games, coaches lose them.' Good start – blame the coach!

A coach must be all things to all players – friend, father-figure, boss, counsellor, judge. He must be honest with players, no matter how difficult it may be. He must be firm but fair. He needs the wisdom of Solomon, the strength of Hercules and the patience of a saint. He must be first at the ground for training and games, and last away. He needs to know each player and what makes that player tick. He must treat all the players the same but each player on his own individual merits. He must know when to deliver his advice and when to hold it back. The coach's smart and tidy manner of dress is important; his knowledge is crucial. Planning of his training/coaching sessions is required in detail. His conditioning programme should be game-related, his sessions varied and interesting. Enjoyment – and hard work – should be the order of the day. The coach must earn the respect of his team.

Coaches fall into many categories: the shouter, the silent, the glory hunter, the ego-tripper, the enthusiast, and the shrewd. The shouter is doomed from the start. He is teaching the team nothing, and if he shouts long enough at his team in time they will switch off. So too is the silent coach doomed. If the coach does not communicate with his team then again they learn nothing. The glory hunter will be in it for himself. He has no thought for his team, his club or the game itself, only for his own personal welfare. He will list winning cups as his yardstick of success, and will blame everyone and everything except himself if he fails. Like the glory hunter, the ego-tripper will destroy the team spirit within the side. The most common type of bad coach, everything will revolve around him and he will be both first and last.

The ideal coach is a mixture of the shrewd and the enthusiastic coach. The enthusiastic coach can, with skill, produce good individual development and a high general team performance. The shrewd coach learns the game thoroughly. He organises his team on both the training area and the football field. He knows his team's weaknessess and its strengths. He finds out about his team's opponents. He communicates with his team and constructively blends individual talents with teamwork. He maintains a good working knowledge and an enthusiastic approach to his coaching.

The good coach must also maintain his own learning process in order to keep up with the various changes that occur from time to time within the skill of coaching. A change in the laws of the game could mean a change in the coach's overall thinking. A great innovation in recent years is the now widely used visual aid of the video cassette. By viewing games other than those of his own team, the modern coach can possibly employ a tactic he sees used by another team. Regarding his own team, the coach can venture into the essential field of video analysis – tackle counts, tackle misses, individual and team mistakes and successes, the kicking game and all aspects of good and bad performances. Pure coaching videos can now be obtained on basic and advanced skills.

Many coaches still cling to the traditional ways taught by 'Old Method' coaches. Some just sit through a game and use memory as their only record. Why not take notes of the points needed for the next coaching session? In order to get a good view of the game a coach might need to move from ground level to an elevated position. He should always be prepared to change his views in other ways, if the change is for the betterment of his team.

An important coaching requirement is a sense of humour. Humour eases tension and can heal wounds often caused unintentionally by a coach in his correction of faults in the individual player. It also introduces a friendly atmosphere within the team as a whole. Laugh with your team, not at them!

The coach must also instil the two prime disciplines of self and team. Not the discipline of the schoolroom — remember we are dealing with footballers, some of whom may be adults — but the sportsman's discipline. Self-discipline includes being fit in body and mind and whenever possible not letting your coach or team down by having a 'rush of blood' and giving away penalties. Team discipline includes working to the game plan, working for the team and training together in all sorts of weather.

Finally, the coach should embrace development and give constructive, positive coaching advice, build character in his individuals and sportsmanship to accept any decision given, work to produce the development of players and of the game of Rugby League Football, and remember that most vital ingredient, enjoyment. Only then will those magic words ring in the coach's ears: 'Here he comes . . . our coach.'

The National Coaching Scheme

The introduction of the Rugby League National Coaching Scheme and its all embracing learning principles has made a tremendous impact on modern coaching techniques. The pyramid of the scheme is structured around three levels of certificate which are obtained by attendance at various courses throughout the year. The theory and practical test to obtain a certificate are both instructional and very enjoyable, and any coach worth his salt should attend. New ideas on training methods, skills practice, football psychology, treatment of injuries, video analysis etc. are regularly taught on the various course levels and many experienced and well-known coaches and players are involved as instructors and pupils.

Before the scheme, it took years of hard-earned experience to be considered for a coaching appointment, at amateur or professional level. While experience is vital even today, the principles of coaching can be learned in a much shorter time thanks to the scheme and a player is never too young to qualify as a coach.

2 Developing the Basic Skills

EQUIPMENT FOR THE COACHING SESSION

In an ideal coaching world several types of equipment will help the coach and players considerably. Most of the following aids to skills practice can be purchased from reputable sports equipment manufacturers and some can also be home-made. For an average 13–18-player session the trainer or coach will need:

1. Eight tackle shields.
2. Four tackle bags.
3. Six rugby balls.
4. Approximately twenty cones or markers.
5. Six large car tyre inner tubes.

Tackle Shields   The tackle shield is a square shield of foam rubber encased in some hard-wearing material, about 0.6 × 0.6 metres with two strips of material forming handles with which to hold the apparatus. This simple protection allows much more physical contact in training, as will be discussed later in this chapter. Much care, though, must be taken in the use of this training aid — the holder of the shield must be aware of the dangers of whiplash action to his neck when a tackler hits the shield, of the clash of heads, and of the tackler's knees hitting him on the thigh and giving him a 'dead leg'.

Tackle Bags   Tackle bags are foam-filled, pear-shaped, free-standing bags, about 1.5 metres high. To the less wealthy clubs an old kitbag packed tightly with rags and paper will do the job.

Rugby Balls   Make sure the balls are pumped up correctly before each session.

Cones or Markers   Cones, or better still the new coloured plastic discs, are needed to mark out your grids.

Car Tyre Inner Tubes   Inner tubes are ideal tackling aids. The metal valve must be covered as protection for the players when in tackling practice, and should be encased in foam rubber, taped well and checked before each session.

The Use of Grids

In physical training and skills practices, grids are simply areas which are smaller than the full pitch or field. Depending on your training or coaching requirements, a grid can be formed by the use of cones, the line markings of the field, or any other marker that shows the grid's size. Working on your skills can be helped by practices in a small area.

Warming up

Warming up must be considered before any coaching or training session. It is essential that every part of the body is prepared for the stresses and strains encountered during the training period. Too often we see players suffer shoulder, neck, back, calf and hamstring injuries during training sessions, usually because not enough time and thought is given to this vital aspect of pre-training build-up. Jogging working up to stride-running, stretching exercises for shoulders, back and legs, shadow-boxing, lifting a partner and fun or enjoyable exercises are a must before serious skills practices at each session. Not just the body but also the mind needs stimulation before each session, so why not include thinking games in your warm-up period? Enjoyment is the key to a good start to your work-out and this will be discussed more fully in Chapter 5.

PASSING AND HANDLING

When passing, the ball should be held with both hands, forming a cradle around the ball. Fingers should be outstretched, holding the ball firmly and in complete control. To transfer the pass to a team mate the passer leans slightly forward from the waist and dips the shoulder nearest the receiver, taking his arms back and then bringing them across his body. The passer's fingers direct the ball, and as the ball leaves the hands the arms follow through towards the receiver. The passer must keep his eyes on the receiver's 'target area', that is a point between chest and hips.

When passing to a running team mate the ball should be directed just in advance of him so that he can run on to the pass. To help direction and accuracy, practise turning the upper body so that both shoulders face the receiver. Never give a forward pass — passing to a team mate in front of you — as this results in loosing vital possession. Do not pass the ball too hard, but weight the

Fig 2   Gary Schofield of Leeds and Great Britain holding the ball in the cradle.

Fig 3   Gary preparing to pass, shoulder dipped nearest the receiver, ball in cradle, eyes on the target area.

Fig 4   Gary's fingers directing the ball, good arm and hand follow-through, eyes still on target area.

Fig 5   Lee Crooks of Leeds and Great Britain, eyes on the ball, elbows slightly bent, fingers open and extended towards the ball.

pass with just enough strength to make the receiver's job so much easier.

When receiving the pass the player must concentrate and keep his eyes on the ball all the way from the passer's hands. He must catch the ball close to his body with both hands. Elbows are slightly bent and fingers are open and extended towards the ball, and as he catches it the receiver cushions the pass into his 'target area', with both hands enveloping the ball safely to his body.

Coaching Points

Passer

1.   Eye on 'target area'.
2.   Good control of ball in hands.
3.   Correctly weighted pass.
4.   Not to a team mate in front of you or in an impossible catching situation.

Fig 6   Catching with both hands, Lee cushions the pass into his target area with hands enveloping the ball safely.

Fig 7   Mike Smith of Hull Kingston Rovers splits the Halifax defence and
continues the move. Note how he keeps his eyes on the supporting
player.

Fig 8   Demonstrating control of the ball in a good passing position, Harry Pinner
looks to continue the move for Great Britain v. New Zealand.

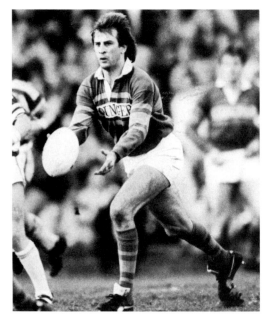

Fig 9 *Marty Gurr, Leeds' Australian fullback, off-loads a super pass against Wigan.*

Receiver
1. Eye on the ball, all the way from the passer's hands.
2. Correct elbow and hand position, using both hands to catch.
3. Pass cushioned into 'target area'.
4. Never over-running the passer.
5. Controlling the ball into a passing position quickly.

Broken Field Passing

This is a pass made with the opponent bearing down directly on the attacker. The attacker must keep his eyes on the receiver and concentrate on weighting his pass correctly if he is to get the ball away to his support successfully. The emphasis here is upon keeping the ball alive.

Fig 10 *Graham Eadie of Halifax off-loads a superb pass despite pressure from a tackle by Kevin Tamati of Warrington.*

Fig 11   Gary Schofield playing for Great Britain keeps his eyes on the receiver despite a hefty tackle from 'Aussie' second row pair Brian Neibling, on the ground, and Wayne Pearce.

Passing under Pressure

This is a pass made by the attacking side whilst under pressure from their opponents. The skill consists in off-loading the pass on the move so that the passer and his support keep going forward.

Passing from the Ground

This is the most common pass from the 'dummy half' or 'acting halfback' position at the play the ball. Vital seconds are lost if the passer picks up the ball, stands upright, then passes. This gives the opposing defence time to run in amongst the line of attack. The correct pass from the ground is given when the passer releases the ball from a crouched position as he unwinds upright. This pass, correctly performed, sets off the attack quickly and accurately.

Fig 12   Colin Maskill of Leeds demonstrates the correct pass from the ground. Note how he keeps his body in a crouched position, eyes on the target and a good cradle hold on the ball.

Fig 13   Still crouched, Colin sends the pass accurately on its way, keeping his eyes on the target.

Fig 14   Once the attack has started the passer then supports, after unwinding from the crouched position.

Coaching Points

1.   Correct position of hands on ball.
2.   Eyes on receiver's 'target area'.
3.   Pass from crouched position.
4.   Correctly weighted pass.

The Drop-Off Pass

An ideal pass to open a defence midfield or worked between centre and wingman. It simply changes the direction of attack. The passer veers across the receiver, sucking the tackler across with him and the receiver times his run inside the passer to hit the hole in the defence which has been created.

Coaching Points

Passer
1.   From a straight run, veer across the receiver.
2.   Head turned to see his 'target area'.
3.   Correctly weighted pass as receiver crosses passer's line of run.

Receiver
1.   Timed inside run.
2.   Not coming inside too early.
3.   Eyes on the ball.
4.   Acceleration into space on receiving ball.

Fig 15   Leeds' international partnership of centre and wing David Stephenson
and John Basnett prepares to perform the drop-off pass. Stephenson,
with the ball, cuts across Basnett's line of run.

Fig 16   Keeping his eyes on the receiver and giving him a good view of the ball,
Stephenson allows Basnett to veer inside him.

Fig 17   Stephenson shields Basnett from the tackler and with his eyes still on
the target off-loads the perfect drop-off pass. Note Basnett's hands
covering the pass.

Fig 18   Away goes Basnett, changing the angle of attack with perfect control of
the ball.

Developing the Basic Skills

The Run Around Pass

This is a passing ploy that can open up any defence, and several variations can be used. The passer, No. 1, off-loads the ball to his team mate, next in line of attack. The receiver, No. 2, catches the ball and watches the original passer run around the back of him, turning to repass as No.1 runs at speed to continue the attack. On receiving the return pass, player No.1 has many options. He could take on the opponents' defence himself, remembering to straighten up his run and not run across the field, or off-load a correctly weighted pass to a supporting team mate.

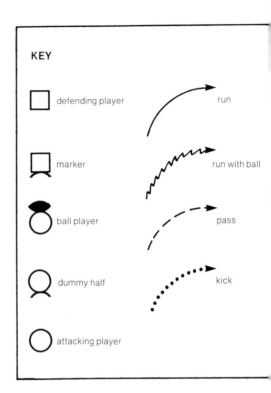

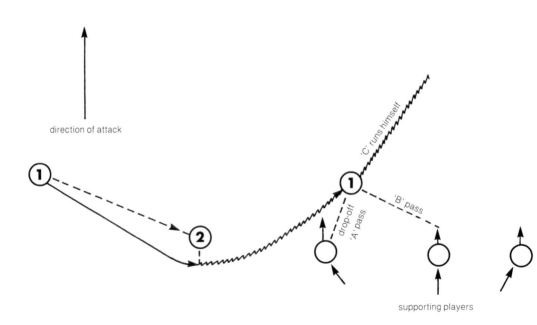

Fig 19   Run around pass options.

Coaching Points

Passer
1. Correctly weighted pass.
2. Eyes on receiver's 'target area'.
3. Run around made quickly.
4. Awareness of supporting players after regaining ball.

Receiver
1. Not running, just taking one step forward.
2. Turning to follow the run around man and watching him all the way.
3. Eyes kept on 'target area'.
4. Correctly weighted pass.

The Double Run Around Pass

This is also very effective on occasions, again with various options as the end product. Passer No. 1 simply off-loads to No. 2, who passes to No. 3. This player waits for No. 1 to run around both No. 2 and himself and weights the pass as in the orthodox run around pass.

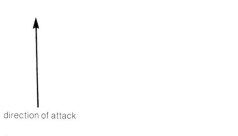

direction of attack

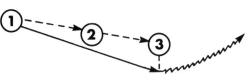

Fig 20   Double run around pass.

Coaching Points

As for Run Around Pass.

The Face Pass

This pass is used to straighten up an attack and changes from normal lateral passing movements to send a runner head on into a gap in the opposing defence. Passer No. 1 simply misses out his team mate No. 2 and weights his pass correctly to hit No. 3 coming on the burst.

Coaching Points

Passer
1. Correctly weighted and timed pass.
2. Pass in front of decoy runner.
3. Eyes on receiver's 'target area'.

Decoy Runner
1. Running from deep position.
2. Not overrunning passer.
3. Appearing to be the one taking the ball up.

Receiver
1. Hitting the pass on the burst.
2. Eyes on the ball all the way from the passer's hands.
3. Awareness of supporting team mates.
4. Prepared to pass if required.

The Miss a Man Pass

This passing ploy is done from a deep-lying position. Passer No. 1 allows his team mate No. 2 to run forward past his line of attack and hits No. 3 with a well-judged pass, which goes behind the running No. 2.

Passing and Handling Practices

The proven modern coaching principles for skills practices are based on small-sided games. This simply means that the particular skill is set in a grid and practised by the individual or in two against one, three against two situations, and so on. Small team games should also be introduced.

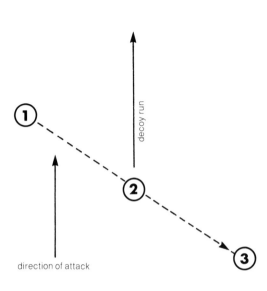

direction of attack

Fig 21   The miss a man pass.

Circle Passing

This is a basic start, where a group of four players, stationary and facing outwards, pass the ball around the circle to their left and, when that is satisfactory, to their right. Circle passing is worked in grids approximately 2 × 2 metres.

Count the Passes

Once the technique of passing and receiving is mastered, a small-sided game of count the passes is advised. In a grid about 7 × 7 metres, Team A has possession and starts with three players against one from Team B. Given about two minutes' game time, Team A counts the number of passes it can string together while challenged by the one member of Team B. The second stage is to increase Team B by one, giving a three against two situation, and finally another Team B member is added to give three against three. The number of passes is counted each time and then the practice is repeated with Team B in possession. The winning team is the one with the most passes. In this practice the ball can be passed in any direction, forwards or backwards, and several games can be going on at the same time in separate grids. The team in possession must move around quickly and take up good catching positions.

Coaching Points

Passer

1.   Letting decoy runner come up level and passing behind him to next man in attacking line.
2.   Eyes on receiver's 'target area'.

Decoy Runner

1.   Timing run correctly.
2.   Not obstructing any defensive player.

Receiver

1.   Eyes on ball all the way from passer's hands.
2.   Taking the pass on the run.
3.   Timing the run correctly.
4.   Prepared to continue the attack by passing if required.

A variation of count the passes is to have Teams A and B in the grid to start with. Team A, in possession, aims to touch any of Team B with the ball (without throwing it at him) whilst both teams are moving around at speed. The player of Team B thus touched must take up the 'leap-frog' position and take no further part until he is released by one of his team mates leaping over him. This is a very enjoyable exercise, which encourages quick and accurate passing.

Double Pass File Running

This is an exercise for eight players and two rugby balls, in a grid about 20 metres long by 8 metres wide. Team members 1 and 2 stand facing each other about 8 metres apart with a ball each, and the remainder of the team stand, line astern, behind No.1 on the start line. At the whistle No.3 runs towards No.1 and calls for the pass with the words 'Short' or 'Wide'. No.1 off-loads the pass correctly to No.3 and immediately looks to No.2 who

passes his ball to him. No.3 runs past No.2 and passes the ball he has received to him. The exercise continues until all the team have gone from start position 'A' and is repeated again from start position 'B' coming in the other direction. It is essential that No.1 has a ball in his hands as quickly as possible at all times to feed the runners and that No.2 releases the ball to No.1 again as quickly as possible so that he can receive the ball back from the runners.

Union Jack

This again involves two rugby balls and eight players, but this time in a 10 × 10 metres grid. Four players stand at the corners of the grid and the other four stand between them, all facing inwards. Players 1 and 5 hold the footballs and at the command 'Go' simultaneously pass the ball clockwise, No.1 to No.2, and No.5 to No.6. As soon as they have passed the balls, they change places with the players opposite by running

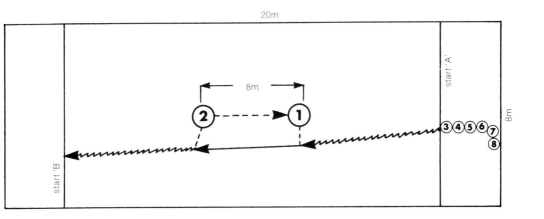

Fig 22   Double pass file running.

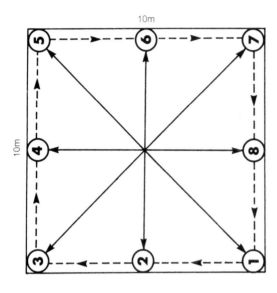

Fig 23   The Union Jack.

across the square diagonally. So after the first pass Nos.1 and 5 change places. Nos.2 and 6 catch the balls and pass them to Nos.3 and 7 respectively and change places, and so on. As No.1 arrives at the No.5 station he receives from No.4. The No.5 player, on arriving at the No.1 station, receives from No.8, and so on. The exercise is repeated for about two minutes, then the players are moved around one place clockwise, thus giving each player the long diagonal run.

PLAY THE BALL

This is the method of bringing the ball back into play after: (a) a tackle; (b) a handover when the team in possession are caught and held after five consecutive play the balls; or (c) the defending team gain possession after a mistake by the attacking team.

The ball must be dropped or placed on the ground in front of the ball player, and then played in any direction by the player bringing his foot in contact with the ball. The usual direction is backwards, thus enabling the player immediately behind him (the 'attacking acting halfback' or 'dummy half') to launch an attack by either passing, running with, or kicking the ball. The remainder of the attacking team must be at least 5 metres behind the line of the ball being played. The defending team is allowed one player (the 'marker') standing directly in front of the ball player; the remainder of the defensive team must be at least 5 metres behind the line of the ball being played, facing the play the ball. The line through the ball is called the 'line of advantage'. This gives a total distance of 10 metres between the attacking and defensive lines.

The ball player, after dropping or placing the ball in front of him, can heel the ball back to his dummy half by placing his playing foot on top of the ball and employing a controlled roll back for the dummy half to pick up. The ball player must keep his body well over the ball because once the ball is placed on the ground the defensive marker is allowed to strike for it with his foot. By keeping well over the ball, the ball player ensures a clean heel for the dummy half, who can then give a perfect pass from the ground

Play the Ball Practices

In groups of four, line astern, about a metre apart directly behind each other, allow the group to practise heeling the ball correctly 1 to 2, 2 to 3, 3 to 4, then turn them around and continue until the ball is back to No.1 This exercise should be practised in the standing position at first and only when each player is proficient at heeling the ball correctly should you progress to players

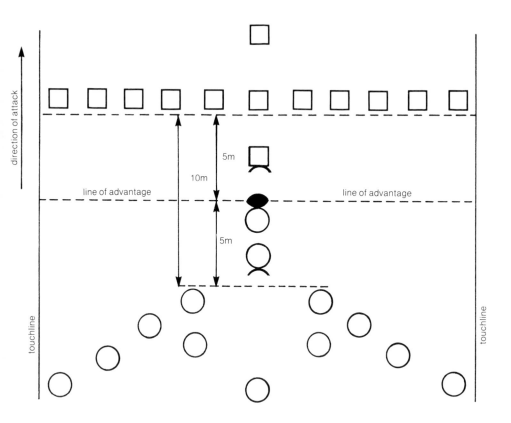

Fig 24   A typical play the ball set-up.

lying in the prone position, as after a ground tackle, regaining their feet as quickly as possible, and then bringing the heeling skill.

Coaching Points

Standing Heel
1.   Ball placed in front of ball player.
2.   Body well over ball.
3.   Sole of playing foot firmly in centre of ball.
4.   Controlled roll by playing foot back to dummy half.

After a Ground Tackle
1.   Regaining feet as quickly as possible.
2.   Facing opponent's goal line.
3.   As for points 1, 2, 3 and 4 above.

Generally allow for ground conditions in the controlled heel back. On a muddy pitch you may need to roll the ball back more firmly than on a dry, level ground. To progress the skill, add a defensive marker to attempt to strike each play of the ball in turn.

Fig 25 Leeds player Richard Gunn places the ball on the ground prior to heeling.

Fig 26 Gunn heels the ball with the sole of his playing foot.

Fig 27 A good, firm, controlled roll back.

Fig 28 The ball is now clear of the ruck. Note the position of Richard Gunn's body well over the ball.

22

Fig 29   Dummy half Maskill awaits the ball from Gunn at the ruck.

Fig 30   Gunn heels, Maskill crouches, Crooks starts his run.

Fig 31   *The ball clear of the ruck, dummy half Maskill glances up at Crooks,
with his hands in a good cradle.*

Fig 32   *The ball is sent on its way by a good passing action from Maskill who
keeps his eyes on Crooks.*

Fig 33   The attack is launched with a good pass away and good play the ball.

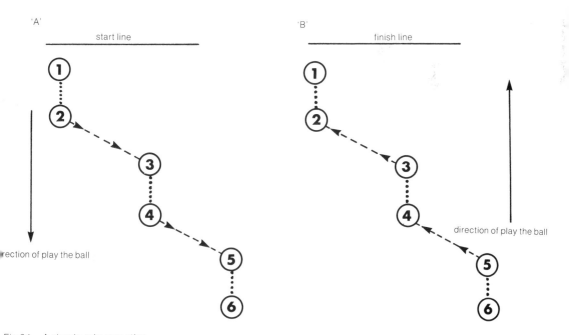

Fig 34   A simple relay practice.

Developing the Basic Skills

Play the Ball and Pass Away from Dummy Half

This is a simple practice done in groups of six and in a grid of about 10 × 10 metres. No.1 plays the ball to No.2, who passes from the ground to No.3, who plays the ball to No.4, who passes to No.5 who plays the ball to No.6. The group then turns around on the spot and repeats the practice in reverse.

Coaching Points

1.   Good controlled heel back to dummy half.
2.   Quick, accurate pass from ground in crouched position.
3.   Tap the ball forward, regather and run only if there is no marker in front of you.

Fig 35   Former Great Britain captain Harry Pinner demonstrates the perfect running control of the ball.

Fig 36   Paul Medley of Leeds demonstrates the same control of the full break this time with a different hold.

RUNNING WITH THE BALL

Running the ball out on attack and keeping control of the football at the same time is a skill that is important to the complete footballer. Too many times we see a player in possession of the football lose the opportunity to continue the attack because he tucks the ball under his arm and just dies in the tackle. When carrying the ball on the run, it should be held in complete control either in both hands or against the chest. Holding in the hands enables the ball carrier to off-load a pass, quickly and accurately to either side of him, and this holding position is suggested when running against a closing defence with support from your team mates. Holding against the chest gives the runner the opportunity to use his free arm to help generate pace or to use in a hand-off, and the ideal time for this holding position is when running clear in a full break.

Running with the Ball Practices

In groups of five, in a grid 30 metres wide by 60 metres long, set up four marker cones, one approximately 6 metres from the grid sideline and the others 6 metres apart and 15 metres behind each other diagonally. From the start line, place player No.1 in line with cone 1, player No.2 in line with cone 2 and so on. Player No.5 will have a clear run on the outside of cone 4 to the finish line. The group runs together and player No.1 attacks cone 1, holding the ball just off his chest with both hands. Approximately one metre from cone 1 he off-loads a pass to player No.2 who attacks cone 2 and brings player No.3 into action, and so on, ending with player

Fig 37   Wilf George of Halifax at full pace but in complete control of the ball.

27

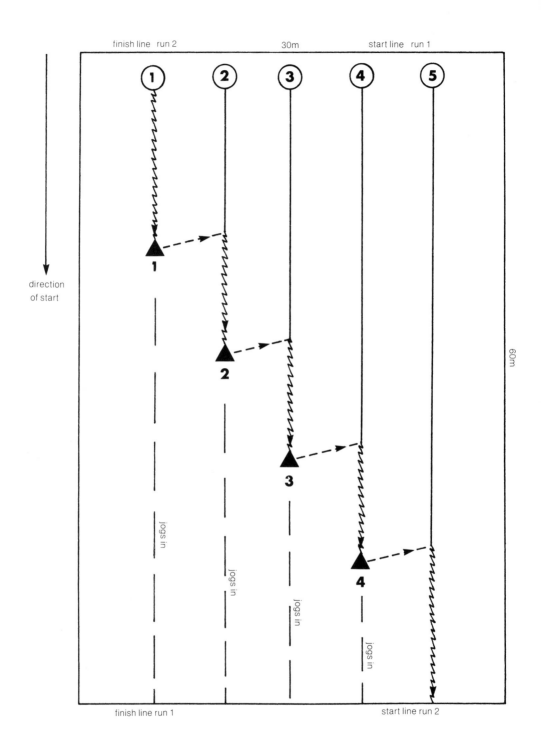

Fig 38   Running with the ball drill.

No.5 running to the end of the grid to complete circuit one. Turn the group around at the finish line and repeat the drill coming the other way, this time player No.5 attacking cone 4, player No.4 running at cone 3 and so on, until player No.1 has the straight run in to the finish line. Adjust the ball-holding position after a while to the one-handed, clean-break carrying position.

Coaching Points

1. Good carrying position of the ball.
2. Controlled, quick adjustment from carrying to passing position of ball.
3. Concentration of passer and receiver.
4. Correct weight of pass, eyes on 'target area'.
5. Study each receiver's skill of catching and eyes on the ball.

SUPPORT PLAY

Each player in any Rugby League team should consider his support play as the most dangerous weapon he possesses. The player should back up any run by his team mates in any sector of the field. Reading the game helps support play. The ability to size up a situation quickly and take up the correct position to receive the ball comes in part from experience but mostly from enthusiasm. Making oneself available to receive the pass stems from keenness and hard work.

Once the support player's awareness is aroused and he has decided where to run when he receives the ball, then he concentrates only on taking the pass from the ball carrier and continuing the attack. To break any line of defence with support play, it is usual for the ball carrier to hit the defensive line, stand up in the tackle and off-load a pass to a support player running close to him. This short support play can be devastating and create many openings, even in international defences. Strength of legs helps considerably when holding off a tackler to transfer the football to a supporting team mate.

Awareness, however, is not enough without communication. Calling for the ball when you are in the correct position is as important as any skill in the game. A bad call, or one that disrupts the passer's concentration, is a breakdown in skills. Do not call for the ball if you are in the wrong position to receive the pass. Good support plus good communication gives a platform for success. A good call gives the ball carrier time to weigh up the opposition's defence and allows him to suck tacklers to

Fig 39   Two all-time greats — 'Aussies' Walley Lewis with the ball, Mal Meninga in support. Big Mal's concentration is there for all to see.

Fig 40   The now famous one—two. Kevin Ward of Castleford holds them up,
          while Andy Gregory of Wigan shows good support in a match for Great
          Britain against Papua New Guinea. Note Ward's eyes on the receiver.

Fig 41   Kevin Ward of Castleford shows leg strength and team mate Bob Linder
          good support against Bradford Northern.

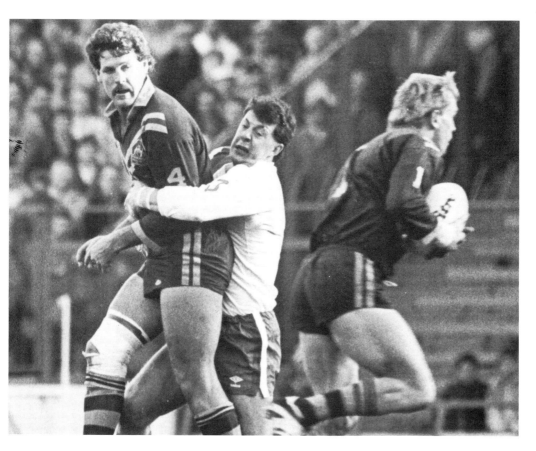

Fig 42   Big Gene Miles of Australia stands in Gary Schofield's tackle and Garry
Jack splits the English defence.

Fig 43   Dale Shearer lets Peter Stirling know he's around as Gary Kemble of
Hull chases the two 'Aussies'.

him before off-loading to the supporting player. Communication needs to be ongoing, not just during play but in the lulls between play.

Support Play Practices

In a grid 10 metres wide by 60 metres long, arrange three sets of two players, each with a tackle shield, down the centre line of the grid. The first two, side by side, stand about 15 metres away from the start line and the second and third pairs at 15-metre intervals. A group of three players form up on the start line in arrowhead formation, the lead man, No.1, carrying the ball. On the command, No.1 runs to burst through the tackle shields 'A' and immediately passes to his left or right to support player No.2 or No.3. The receiver times his support run, communicates with the passer, takes the pass and runs at tackle shields 'B' with player No.1 taking the runner's place in support. The runner bursts through shields 'B' and passes on his left or right to either player in support, who then attacks shields 'C' while the runner takes the support position. After completing the first circuit, simply turn the shield carriers on the spot and repeat the drill coming the opposite way.

Channel Support Play Practice

In the same grid, place four players holding tackle shields. These players can run about at will and can check or block the runners physically with the shields. Against these four shield men, place five players carrying the ball. Their objective is to support the ball carrier and score a try at the end of the grid. Timing of the support run is vital and this drill, with its stop—go action, instils that timing factor in the supporting man's play.

Grid-Iron Rugby

This support play drill is very popular with players, and consists of a game of touch football played in a grid 50 metres wide by 68 metres long (half of a rugby pitch), working in seven-a-side groups. The ball can be passed in any direction, to the side, backwards or forwards, and the object is for the attacking team to score a try by almost non-stop passing and supporting play. The touches are unlimited and on scoring a try the attacking team gives up the ball and the defending team regains possession to attack from their own goal line.

Coaching Points

1. Concentration in delivery of the pass.
2. Timing of the run into the support position.
3. Concentration on receiving the ball.
4. Continuity of attack from support play.

REGAINING POSSESSION

As in passing and handling, and in running with the ball, control of the football is crucial when picking up a dead or rolling ball and dropping on a stationary or moving ball. The basic principle of skill is the same for controlling either the rolling or motionless ball. On picking up a ball the player keeps his eyes on it and straddles it with his feet, one foot slightly in front and the other behind. Without breaking stride he stoops and picks it up with both hands, one on the front half of the ball and the other on the rear half. Finally, he brings the ball into the carrying position and continues the attack. In dropping on a loose ball the principles do not change. The player keeps his eyes on the ball and, as he drops on to it, he covers the

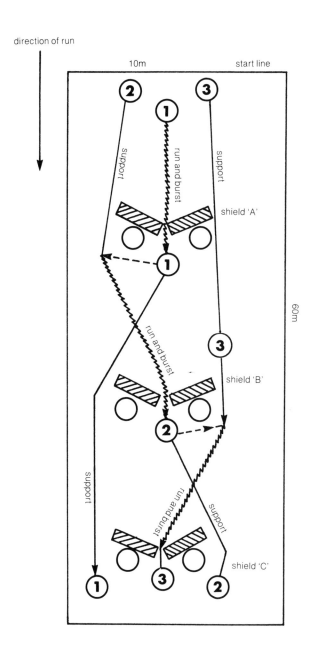

direction of run

10m

start line

support

run and burst

support

shield 'A'

60m

run and burst

shield 'B'

support

run and burst

support

shield 'C'

Fig 44   Arrowhead support drill for three players.

Fig 45 Lee Crooks approaches the pick-up with feet and hands in the correct position.

Fig 47 Crooks runs on his way, holding on to the ball safely.

Fig 46 In full control, Crooks safely regains possession.

ball with his body and gains control with his hands.

Picking-Up Practices

The Still Ball

Place two marker cones 5 metres apart in line astern in a grid 5 metres wide by 20 metres long. From the start line, the player runs at a ball at the side of the front marker. He picks up the ball, running at speed, replaces it on the ground at the second marker, and sprints to the finish line. He then turns and repeats the exercise coming the other way. He should practise picking up the ball from both left and right.

The Rolling Ball

In the same grid, place another player with a football along with the skills practising player. The latter starts running and from

Fig 48   Marty Gurr weighs up the ball.

Fig 49   Gurr drops on to the ball with control.

Fig 50   Hiding the ball from the opponent's view, Gurr regains possession.

the grid sideline the player with the ball rolls the football into his path. He stoops, picks up the ball on the run and continues to the finish line. Returning the ball to the roller, he then repeats the exercise coming the other way. By moving the roller to the other side of the grid, the player can practise the exercise from both sides. This exercise can also be varied to allow the practice of picking up a ball rolling towards and away from the player.

Dropping on the Ball Practices

These can be practised using the same basic method as the various picking up drills. But instead of picking up the ball, the practising player drops on the ball from the side, from the front, chasing back with the ball rolling

away from him, and in the dead-ball situation.

Coaching Points

1.   Control of the ball.
2.   Concentration on approach to picking up or dropping on ball.
3.   When picking up, correct leg and hand positions.
4.   When dropping on, covering the ball with the body and controlling with the hands.

EVASIVE TACTICS

The Hand-Off

This is a method of evading a tackle which is used by most players, and is a straight-arm

Fig 51   Howie Tamati, No. 2, hands off fellow Kiwi Gordan Smith of Hull Kingston Rovers.

thrust, with open palm, usually against the head, chest or face of the attempting tackler, but sometimes against his arm or shoulder. Do not hand off with the clenched fist as this is illegal. It is very important to carry the ball in the correct hand during the hand-off. A left winger, for instance, should carry the ball cushioned to his chest by his left hand, to allow his inside arm to be used for the hand-off; a right winger in his right hand. The practice of changing hands in the holding position while running should be encouraged as it gives the runner the skill to hand off one tackler coming from his left, the next from his right and so on.

The Side Step

The side step, or changing direction, is an evasive tactic that can be used by forwards or backs. When faced by a tackler, the runner attempts to turn him one way, then steps across his line to accelerate away. If the side step is to the tackler's left, the runner would veer slightly across to the tackler's right and then, about 1 metre from the tackler, would thrust his left foot hard into the ground and prop strongly back to his own right. The same basics apply in side stepping to the tackler's right: the runner's right foot is thrust into the ground and he props across to his left. It is of great

Fig 52   John Basnett of Leeds fends off Deryk Pyke of Leigh.

Fig 53   Lee Crooks of Leeds evades a Leigh opponent, No. 13, with a short side
step. Note how the Leigh player's body has been made to lean away
from the tackle by Crooks's feint and thrust with his stepping leg. Gary
Spencer is in support.

advantage to be able to side step either way, left or right.

The Dummy

This is a ploy to make the defender think a pass is intended. The runner goes through the motions of passing but retains possession of the ball without off-loading the pass. The runner must keep his eyes on the player to whom he apparently intends to pass in order to deceive the tackler.

Hit and Spin

In this tactic the runner heads straight at a defender and as the tackler stoops to effect the tackle the runner, if breaking to his left, plants his left foot directly in front of the stooping tackler, dips his left shoulder into the defender and thrusts forward, at the same time spinning completely around to his left and using the tackler as a buffer. He can either spin out of the tackle and continue his run, or off-load a pass to a man in support. If spinning to his right, the right foot comes forward, the right shoulder bumps the tackler and he pivots around to his right.

The Change of Pace

The object of the change of pace is to slow down the tackler's movements. The runner slows down his own speed and as the tackler eases into his tackle the runner accelerates away at full speed.

The Swerve

This method of evading a tackle takes the runner in an arc around the tackler. If the defender is coming in quickly from an angle the runner simply veers across the line of the tackle on the inside. If a defending player is coming across in a slower motion, weighing up the runner, the runner's arc is then on the outside.

Evasive Tactics Practices

The Hand-Off

In a grid approximately 10 metres wide by 40 metres long, place four players holding tackle shields. Stagger them, two to each of the long sides of the grid, about 9 metres apart behind each other and facing the start line. The runner attacks shield 1 at speed and hands off the shield. To allow him to hand off with his free arm, he then changes the ball-holding position whilst running at speed and attacks shield 2. This continues until he has completed the circuit at the finish line.

Coaching Points

1.   Strong, straight-arm hand-off, thrusting the tackler off balance.
2.   Controlled change of ball-carrying position whilst running at speed.
3.   Acceleration away from hand-off.

The Side Step

Set up a grid 20 metres wide by 60 metres long and place six cones in two rows of three as shown in Fig. 55. The practising player runs at speed and performs the side-step drill at each cone in turn, off his left foot on the first circuit and off his right on the second. When the runner is proficient, replace the cones with players to increase pressure.

Coaching Points

1.   A slight veer across the front of the cone.

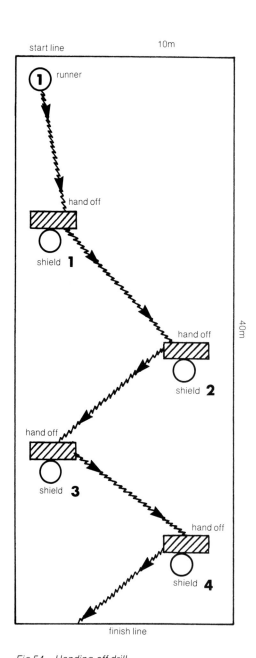

Fig 54   Handing-off drill.

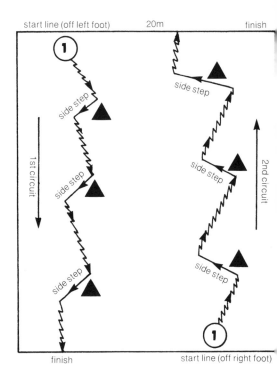

Fig 55   Side step drill.

2.   A big thrust by the propping foot back across the line of cone.

3.   Acceleration away to side step the next cone.

The Dummy

Practices for this evasive tactic can be performed in any handling practice or game of touch rugby.

Coaching Points

1.   Going through exact motion as in passing.

2.   Eyes on the dummy receiver.

3.   Holding on to the ball to the last instant before passing.

4.   Acceleration into gap caused by dummy.

Hit and Spin

Set up four tackle shields and holders in a grid 10 metres wide by 30 metres long. The four shields are in line astern of each other but staggered diagonally. Player No.1 runs at speed against shield 1, dips his right shoulder into the shield, hits, spins and attacks shield 2, and repeats the exercise until he finishes the circuit. Coming the other way down the grid, he hits and spins to the left with his left shoulder. To add support play, simply introduce another player to support player No.1. As No.1 spins, the support player times his run, communicating with No.1, and receives the pass to attack shield 2. Player No.1 now becomes the support player and so on.

Coaching Points

1.   Right shoulder dipped into tackler to spin right.
2.   Left shoulder dipped into tackler to spin left.
3.   Awareness of supporting team mates and passing possibilities during pivot.
4.   Spinning out of tackle and continuing run.

The Swerve

In a narrow grid 5 metres wide by 20 metres long, practise arc running between opposite corners, swerving from left to right, and to left again, using the full width. To swerve to the left, the right leg comes across the running line and the body leans slightly left. To swerve to the right, the left leg comes across the running line. Two more players may be introduced as defenders, allowing the runner to practise swerving both ways.

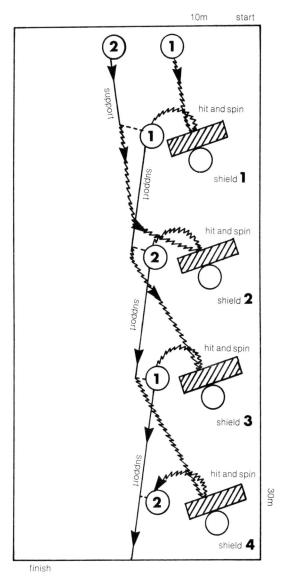

Fig 56   Hit and spin drill, with support.

Coaching Points

1.   Right leg across running line to swerve left.
2.   Left leg across running line to swerve right.
3.   Encourage body to lean away from tackler during swerve.
4.   Acceleration during and after swerve.
5.   Awareness of support players.

SCRUMMAGING

A scrum is formed by six men from each side as a method of bringing the ball back into play from a knock-on or forward pass, or when the ball goes out of play from a broken field kick, etc. The referee will give the mark where he wants the scrum to be formed by raising his arms aloft and touching his

Fig 58   The hooker, Colin Maskill, places his arms over his prop's shoulders.

Fig 57   Leeds prop forwards Lee Crooks, right, and Mark Brooke-Cowden binding from front.

Fig 59   The second row pair Gary Price, No.11, and Kevin Rayne, No.12, bind as shown.

fingertips together like an umbrella above his head.

The two prop forwards, No.8 on the open side and No.10 on the blind side, bind together on the referee's mark. The hooker, No.9, binds between the props with his arms over and around their necks, giving a tight and solid front row. The second-row pair, No.11 and No.12, bind together before they enter the scrum. The open-side second row, No.11, grips his partner over and around his shoulders, while the blind-side second row grips around his partner's waist. Both then enter their heads into the scrum and place their shoulders under the buttocks of the hooker and props, attaining a good pushing position with their backs level with the ground, outside legs bent to push and inside legs back to form a channel for the ball to roll through. The lock or loose forward, No.13, then enters his head between the second

Fig 60   Second row in the scrum. Note the position of the legs.

Fig 61   Second row's backs level with the ground, legs forming a channel for the ball to roll through.

Fig 62   *Loose forward Richard Gum, No.13, locks the scrum at the rear.*

row, placing his shoulders under their buttocks and spreading his legs to control the wheeling of the scrum.

At a typical scrummage the referee will stand on the open side of play. The other side of the scrum is called the 'blind side'. The player who rolls the ball into the scrummage tunnel is called the scrum half. He must roll the ball dead in centre of the tunnel and not give his hooker unfair advantage, and then he must immediately retire behind his loose forward. The opposing scrum half must stay behind the line of his loose forward until the ball emerges from the scrum and is back in play. The ball is in play when it comes out behind the feet of either of the second-row pair. Any of the front row may strike for the ball with their feet once the ball has entered the

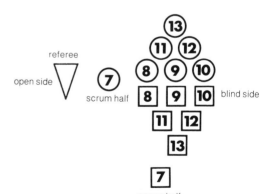

Fig 63   *A typical scrum formation.*

scrum tunnel. Both packs or forwards may push once the ball has entered the tunnel.

If the ball is won at the scrum, the loose forward must support any break by his backs. The second-row pair must also break from the scrum quickly and be ready to continue the attack by support play. The winning front row must rejoin the attack as quickly as possible.

If the ball is lost at the scrum, the lock or loose forward must first check quickly to see if the opposition are attacking the blind side and if they are not he covers, at speed, across the back of his defending three-quarters. The second-row men trail across with the loose forward and behind him. The front row must work hard to get from the scrum to a defensive station around the next play the ball ruck as soon as possible.

Scrummaging Practices

Plenty of practice is required in scrummaging. Practise your forwards against your backs on training night; it is good fun and also makes the backs realise the physical pressures on the forwards. Also practise the various forward positions breaking from the scrum both on attack and defence. These drills can be practised in different areas of the full-sized pitch. Cover tackling for loose and second-row forwards can be practised by scrummaging near a touchline and having the backs move the ball away, the open-side backs acting as the opposition's attack while your back three forwards cover across.

Coaching Points

In the Scrum
1.   Good tight binding with correct leg positions.

2.   All the backs of the pack parallel to the ground.
3.   Good united push after ball has entered scrum.

When Ball is Won
1.   Lock and second row out quickly to support.
2.   Front row away as quickly as possible.

When Ball is Lost
1.   Loose forward checks blind side and for possible attack.
2.   If no attack loose forward covers out, open side, behind his backs.
3.   Second row out quickly to cover behind loose forward.
4.   Front row around the next play the ball, in defence, as soon as possible.

TACKLING

This aspect of play is vital to the success of a team or an individual player. The techniques of tackling are simple and effective if the basic principles are adhered to. In tackling, as in passing and handling, the tackler must keep his eyes on the 'target area', which in tackling is usually between the waist and knees of the runner. One must always tackle with the utmost determination — never attempt a half-hearted tackle as that is when major injuries occur. Tackle with confidence, determination and the correct skills, and the defensive side of your game will become easy. In fact you will enjoy tackling.

The Side Tackle

This is a common tackle used hundreds of times each season by all players. The tackler's eyes are kept on the 'target area'

Fig 64   Brooke-Cowden sizes up Rayne and approaches to tackle.

Fig 65   Brooke-Cowden hits the target with his shoulder.

Fig 66   The tackler puts his arms around the legs of the runner.

Fig 67   The tackler drives from his legs into the runner.

Fig 68   This Hunslet second row No. 11 brings down Roy Dickinson of Leeds
          and Great Britain.

Fig 69   Lee Crooks, then of Hull, stops Castleford's 'Aussie' Ronnie Sigsworth.

and the runner is approached at speed and with determination. Hitting the 'target area' with his leading shoulder his head always behind the runner's buttocks, the tackler wraps both arms around the runner's thighs and knocks him to the ground with a powerful drive of both legs.

The Rear Tackle

This tackle is also approached with determination and again with eyes on the 'target area'. Arms clasped tightly around the thighs, the tackler's legs drive the runner down to the ground and the tackler ends up on top of the runner's legs.

The Front-On Passive Tackle

This is about the most widely used weapon in defence, and is the ideal tackle for a smaller player to bring down a bigger opponent. The tackler confronts the runner head-on, in a crouched position and with his eyes on the runner's 'target area'. With his head to the side of the runner, the tackler blocks the runner's thighs with his leading shoulder and his arms embrace the thighs tightly. On contact the tackler simply falls backwards, remaining in the crouched position and maintaining his hold of the runner's thighs. The runner's own momentum brings him to the ground and the tackle is completed with both tackler and runner firmly locked together on the ground.

Fig 70   Gunn approaches Brooke-Cowden, eyes on target.

Fig 71   Here we see Gunn adopting a good tackling position, head to the side,
         good leg drive, arms around runner's legs.

Fig 72   The tackle is now almost complete. Note the head position of the tackler.

Fig 73 A well-executed tackle with the tackler on top.

Fig 74 Gary Price blocks Colin Maskill and falls backwards.

Fig 75 Maskill's own momentum brings him down with Price holding on.

Fig 76   The tackle complete, Price is still
          locked on to Maskill.

Fig 77   Kelvin Skerrett, then of Hunslet, halted
          by a good drive tackle.

This tackle is not recommended near one's
own try line as the runner could easily reach
out and score a try. The front-on passive
tackle is ideal in midfield or near the
attacker's own try line.

The Block or Drive Tackle

This is a very destructive method of
stopping a runner dead in his tracks. The
'target area' in this case is the runner's
midriff. The tackler hits the runner with his
leading shoulder, head to the side, and with
his legs slightly bent at the knee. The
tackler's arms envelop the runner's thighs
with his hands placed under the runner's
buttocks. On contact, the tackler drives
slightly upwards with his legs and, still
holding firmly with his arms, turns the
runner on to his side, on the ground.

Fig 78   Mick Burke of Widnes stopped by the
          driving Lee Crooks, then of Hull.

Fig 79   Clash of the giants as Big Bren Hill of Bradford Northern creams Kevin
Ward of Castleford.

The 'Blockbuster' Tackle

This is the most devastating stopper in the book and is recommended for use near one's own try line. The tackler approaches the runner head-on, his leading shoulder blocks the runner's thighs, head to the side, and his arms envelop and grip the runner's legs behind his knees. The tackler's own knees are slightly bent and on contact the tackler uses his legs as springs, straightening them in his drive up and back.

The runner's feet are lifted from the ground as the tackler continues his drive forward still gripping firmly behind the runner's knees. The tackler maintains his momentum and dumps the runner backwards into the ground.

Fig 80   Marty Gurr of Leeds about to go up
and back in this Halifax blockbuster.
Note the tackler's leg position.

Fig 81   Rayne sets up Price.

Fig 82   The tackler keeps his head to the side and drives off his legs with his
arms firmly around the runner.

Fig 83   The runner is put off balance, going backwards.

Fig 84   Going down. The tackle is complete.

The Smother Tackle

This is the only tackle performed in an upright stance and can be used in midfield, near either try line or in a defensive position facing two opponents. The object is to trap the ball between the runner's and tackler's bodies thus stopping the runner passing the ball. The tackler sizes up the runner head-on and keeps his eyes on him. Approaching the runner at speed, the tackler embraces him, head to side, his arms around the runner's chest and gripping his hands tightly on his opponent's back. The ball is thus trapped between his and the runner's chests. Holding on firmly, the tackler turns the runner around to his side and forces him to the ground, finishing up on top of the grounded runner.

Individual and Team Tackling Practices

Defence is a very important skill. The individual practices of the various tackles must be worked on hard, but it is not enough to have thirteen good tacklers on your team; that defence needs to be organised into defensive teamwork.

The Side Tackle

For both the side tackle and rear tackle practices, inflated inner tubes are a superb practice aid, helping to build confidence and technique without fear of injury. Set up a grid 10 × 10 metres and station four players with an inner tube each at the corners. Place one player in the centre of the grid,

Fig 85   Maskill approaches Crooks.

Fig 86   Maskill traps the ball between their bodies.

Fig 87   The tackler grips his opponent in an embrace.

Fig 88   Maskill turns Crooks in the tackle.

Fig 89   The tackler forces the runner to the ground.

A simple four-against-four side tackle practice is to set up a grid 10 metres wide by 20 metres long. At point 'A' place four players each with a ball. At point 'B' place the remaining four players facing across the grid. Both sets of four players are line astern to each other. At the command, player No. 1 starts his run down the centre of the grid and player No. 2 comes in from the side and performs the side tackle. They exchange the football, player No. 1 quickly retires to the back of point 'B', behind player No. 2 and player No. 8, and then runs with the ball behind player No. 7. When the grid has been cleared of players for No. 3's run the practice continues until all four tackles are complete and all the roles are reversed.

Fig 90   Ian Potter of Wigan and Great Britain smother tackles George Fairburn of Hull Kingston Rovers.

facing tube 1, having numbered the tube rollers 1 to 4 for the benefit of the tackler. On the command, tube 1 is rolled firmly across the grid diagonally. The tackler times his side tackle to hit the tube in the prescribed manner. The roller of tube 1 quickly retrieves his tube and the second tube is then rolled across the grid. The practice is repeated until the tackler has completed four tackles, one on each tube. He then takes the first tube position and the former roller of tube 1 becomes the tackler. After his four practices he takes over from the roller of tube 2 who becomes the tackler, and so on until the practice is complete with each player having taken a turn as tackler. This practice can be progressed by exchanging inner tubes for running players carrying a ball. The grid must be clear of runner No. 1 before runner No. 2 starts, thus giving the tackler time to recover and make the following tackle perfectly.

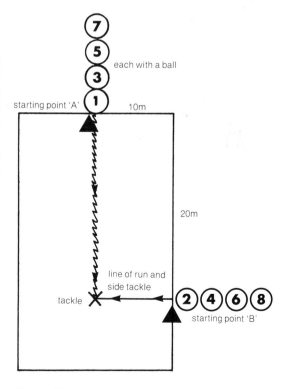

Fig 91   The side tackle.

The Rear Tackle

The rear tackle can be practised with an inner tube in a grid 5 metres wide by 10 metres long. Tube roller No. 1 stands with the tube facing tube roller No. 2 at the opposite end of the grid. The tackler stands beside roller No.1 who rolls the tube firmly for him to chase and tackle. Roller No. 2 retrieves the tube, returns to his station, and when the tackler has recovered and is ready to go again, rolls the tube back to roller No. 1. The tackler repeats the exercise, tackling the tube before it reaches roller No. 1.

Further pressure can be applied with four tubes on a grid 10 metres wide by 15 metres long. On the start line place four tube rollers about 3 metres apart with the tackler behind tube 1. This is rolled firmly forwards and the tackler chases and tackles it. The tackler quickly runs behind tube 2 and repeats the practice until he has completed the circuit by tackling all four tubes. The tube roller retrieves his tube quickly after the tackle is completed and returns to his station on the start line. After his four tackles the tackler takes up the tube 1 position, and the former holder of tube 1 becomes the tackler. After his practice he takes tube 2 and the former holder of tube 2 makes his four tackles, and

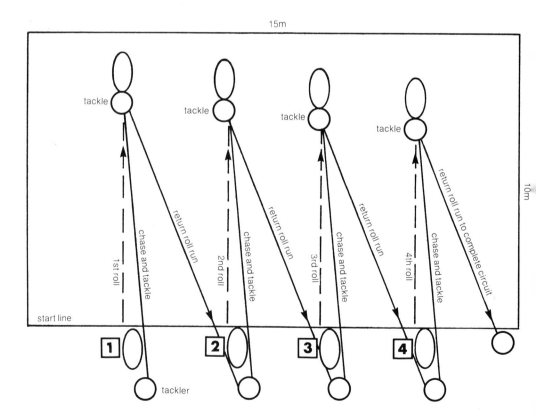

Fig 92   The rear tackle (with tubes).

so on. A further extension of this practice is simply to exchange the tubes for running players.

The Front-On Passive Tackle

Tubes should also be used in the practice of the front-on passive tackle. In a grid 2 metres wide by 5 metres long, a tube roller is placed at the start line and a tackler is placed directly in front of the tube 5 metres away. The tube is rolled firmly at the tackler, who positions himself in the crouched stance, head to the side, and blocks the tube with his leading shoulder. On contact the tackler falls over backwards and, with a firm grip on the tube, retains control of the tackle with the tube held on the ground. The tackler regains his feet and returns the tube down the grid, enabling the other player to practise the tackle. Again this practice can be extended using a running player who is carrying a ball.

The Block or Drive Tackle

Tackle bags are ideal aids in the practice of both the drive tackle and the blockbuster tackle. In the drive tackle the tackler attacks the bag, which is held by a team mate who releases his hold on contact. The tackler hits the bag, head to the side, and with his arms gripping tightly around the bag he drives slightly upwards and turns the bag in mid-tackle to finish up on top of the bag.

The 'Blockbuster' Tackle

In the blockbuster tackle, the principle of the drive tackle is repeated, but instead of turning the bag in mid-tackle, the tackler lifts the bag in his follow-through and continues his drive forward, dumping the bag on the ground and landing on top of it. There is no need to work this practice in a grid but

ensure that there is plenty of space between bags if in group practice. Avoid this practice on uneven or barren ground; a well-grassed surface or soft gym matting is ideal.

A good conditioning/skills exercise in most tackling drills is to place a football about a metre away from the inner tube or tackle bag. After completing the tackle correctly, the player is required to drop immediately on to the football to practise regaining possession of a loose ball. Joint skills drills like this help players to develop the ability to gather a ball released by tackling.

Coaching Points

In All Tackles
1.   Eyes on the tackle target.
2.   Head to the side of target.
3.   Driving with leading shoulder.
4.   Arms taking firm grip.
5.   Driving with legs.
6.   Always tackling with determination.

KICKING SKILLS

The Orthodox Punt

Possibly the most common of all the kicks, the punt is used in a variety of situations during a game. Its main function is to gain ground for your team in an organised and practised kicking game plan. It can also be used to find touch from a penalty awarded to your team, either if you decide against kicking at goal from a full penalty or if you are awarded a differential penalty. In broken field play the punt is generally used to kick down or slightly across field for position, not only on the last tackle but also when needed to fit into your kicking game plan.

Some teams will kick immediately they

Fig 93   Gary Schofield holds the ball for a
          punt.

Fig 94   With his eyes on the ball and arms out
          for balance, Gary prepares to strike.

Fig 95   Gary keeps his head down, eyes on
          the ball, striking with the instep.

Fig 96   Swinging hip follow-through, head still down,
          eyes still on the ball.

Fig 97   Good, high, balanced follow-through.

gain possession in certain areas of the field. Imagine winning a scrum about 10 metres from your own line. Your scrum half passes to your stand-off half, who kicks, deep and long, downfield. A good chasing game by your three-quarters puts the opposition under pressure immediately by having them scurry back towards their own line with your backs breathing down their necks. But the kick is no good without the chasers, and the old saying is very true indeed, 'If you don't chase, then don't kick.'

Gaining ground by a downfield punt is one thing, but punting to gain touch with a bounce is another. Your kicker needs a tremendous amount of practice before he starts knocking those fifty yarders towards touch. When kicking for the side line, most kickers are inclined to be too greedy and attempt, without much practice, to gain that extra little bit of ground. Consequently, we either see a nice kick land in the field of play but without control of the bounce, so that the opposition regains possession directly, or

the ball goes out on the full, producing a scrummage for the opponents where the kicker attempted his 'greedy' kick.

The kicker must know before he kicks where the ball will end its flight, and he must be aware of how far downfield he wants the ball to go. Good practice will tell a kicker his maximum length, but he must also take weather conditions into account. From a stationary kick the kicker must look to where he intends the ball to land, and cradle the ball as if for passing. He then backs off from the mark of the kick and, keeping his eyes on the ball, simply pours it from his hands upon reaching the mark. With his arms out-stretched for balance and his eyes still on the ball, he strikes it with the instep of his kicking foot and with his head still down punches the kicking leg through from the hip, completing the punt with a high follow-through.

The Up-and-Under Kick

The up-and-under kick, or bomb, is a ploy much used near the opponent's try line, and needs to be very accurate as overkicking may send the ball directly over the dead-ball line and out of play. The ball is kicked high in the air to allow the kicker or his team mates to gain position. Everyone in the team must be behind the kicker at the moment of impact to keep them on-side. The kick is also best placed just in the field of play, but not in the in-goal area — remember that, if an opponent catches the ball on the full in his own in-goal area, his side is allowed to restart the game with a tap-kick from the centre of its 22-metre line.

The Chip or Kick Over

This is a particularly effective ploy when faced by a defence that is moving up very

Fig 98   Terry Webb, former Leeds and
          Hunslet Australian forward, shows the
          correct technique for the bomb kick.

Fig 99   Gurr of Leeds hits a perfect spiral
          punt.

quickly. The kicker simply chips or punts the ball over the heads of the defence, either for himself or a team mate to chase. The area at which to aim is the no man's land between the front line of defence and the fullback. Judgement of weight, length and height of kick again requires practice. The emphasis is on height rather than length.

The Spiral or Torpedo Punt

This kick sends the ball spinning lengthways through the air, in an aerodynamic way rather like a bullet leaving a gun. The ball is held, for a right-footed kicker, with the right hand at the top point of the football and the left hand at the bottom point, with the ball at an angle of around 45 degrees across the body. When the ball is poured down, the kicking foot imparts spin by kicking across or slicing the ball. In flight the football spirals away and is inclined to spin across to the kicker's left. This kick gives more length

than the normal punt kick, and it is more difficult to catch in flight as its movement through the air and its spinning motion can confuse the catcher.

The spiral punt is the hardest of the punt kicks to master. Lots of practice, and many miskicks in practice, will be required before this most effective weapon is controlled, but sticking with it will soon develop the confidence to use this kick in the kicking game plan.

The Grubber Kick

Either midfield or near your opponent's try line, the grubber kick is a devasting ploy with which to turn or break a defence. It can also be used to gain ground in tactical touch-finding. In the grubber the ball is kicked along the ground, end over end. The ball is held as for passing, then poured down from the hands, with the body slightly leaning over the ball. As the ball touches the ground

Fig 100   Schofield pours the ball down.

Fig 101   The kicking foot comes forward in a stabbing motion, the head and
body are kept over the ball.

Fig 102   The kicking foot is stabbed into the ground and punched through.

Fig 103   The ball on its way, the body of the kicker is still leaning forward and the head is still kept down.

Fig 104   The kick is completed with the player still in an ideal position.

the instep of the kicking foot stabs the ball into the ground and punches it along the ground. The leaning of the body, the stabbing, kicking action and the low follow-through help control the kick and ensure a low, end-over-end, accurate grubber kick. At the end of the kick, the head should still be down, the body lean still in evidence, the kicking foot pointing in the direction of the kick, and the kicker well-balanced.

The Drop Kick

This is possibly the least used of all the kicks, probably because of the skill required to drop kick accurately. It is used to restart play under the posts or from the 22-metre line, after the ball has been made dead inside the in-goal area or after the opposition has missed a penalty kick at goal. It is used most obviously to gain one point from the drop goal during broken field play. A team can gain two points from a penalty drop kick at goal.

For the drop kick, the football is held in the passing position or cradle. It is poured from the hands to the ground and struck with the instep of the kicking foot on the half volley or just as the point of the ball touches the ground. The arms, the kicking leg and the body position determine the height, length and direction of the drop kick. The arms are outstretched for balance, the kicking leg strikes through the ball with a good, high follow-through, and the body leans slightly backwards to give height to the kick. The head should stay down during the kick with the kicker's eyes on the ball.

In any game plan it is vital to be able to call on a good drop kicker. Many games are lost by a team's failure to use this skill to gain the one point score. The drop kicker can also relieve pressure when a team is forced to drop out from under its posts or from its

Fig 105 *Schofield pours the ball down, keeping his eyes on it.*

Fig 107 *The body leans slightly back for a high kick with good follow-through and balance.*

Fig 106 *Gary strikes a half-volley with the instep, keeping his head down.*

22-metre line, and good chasing following a long drop out can turn a game.

The Place Kick

A good place kicker is also worth his weight in gold. Place kicks from the centre spot are used to start the game and to restart it after a score, but the most common use of place kicks is in kicking at goal or into touch from a penalty or attempting to convert a try. Some teams place kick to touch instead of punting and this is quite legal. During a game the place kicker must have full confidence in his own ability. He must know also the limits of his place kick: to miss a penalty kick at goal because the distance is too far is an indication of a terrible decision by kicker or captain.

There are two types of place-kicking technique. One is the 'round the corner' approach, striking the dead ball, soccer fashion, with the full instep of the kicking

Fig 108   Placing the ball on the tee.

Fig 109   Addressing the ball.

foot. The other mode of strike is straight on to the football, kicking with the toe of the foot. This second method is now somewhat outdated, perhaps because striking the ball with the instep gives less margin of error than kicking with the toe. Some experts, though, consider that the 'round the corner' kick has a natural swing in flight which means that it is only suitable for right-footed kickers on the left side of the field and vice versa. The toe-end kicker, on the other hand, kicks through the line of the ball and so does not have a 'bad' side of the field. Look at both types of kick during practice and use the method that suits your requirements.

In the 'round the corner' place kick, it is advisable to tee up the ball on a small pyramid of sand. Making sure the ball is placed correctly on the tee in relation to the posts, it is addressed by placing the non-kicking foot at the side of the ball and the kicking foot in the position of strike. The usual method for determining the starting-point for the run-up is to back off the ball to the required distance then (if right-footed) take several steps to the left. The kicker should check once again that the angle and length of run are correct, and should concentrate on the spot of kick, the line of flight and the follow-through. Fixing his eyes on the ball the kicker gains momentum in his run-up, approaches the kick with confidence and, with arms out for balance, comes in at the correct angle to sweep the ball over the crossbar and through the posts. At point of contact the eyes should still be on the striking point, the head down and the body leaning back slightly. The follow-through should be a natural and free swing of the kicking leg from the hip, high and slightly across the body line.

The toe-end kick preparation is similar in many ways. The ball is teed up on sand and

Fig 110   The player is ready for the run up to the kick.

Fig 111   The player takes a final stride, eyes on the spot of the kick.

Fig 112   The ball is sent on its way while the head remains down, and the player leans slightly backwards.

70

Fig 113   *The follow-through.*

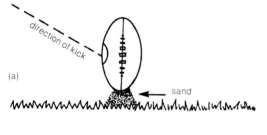

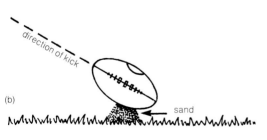

Fig 114   *Place-kicking tees (a) upright kick
(b) torpedo kick.*

addressed as before. The kicker then backs off to his required length of run-up, approaches with acceleration and punches straight through the ball with the kicking foot, using a strong natural swing of the kicking leg through from the hip and keeping the head down. For longer kicks, the ball may be teed up like a torpedo, with the back point of the ball raised up off the ground and facing the kicker, and the front point facing the posts. This ensures lift and height in the kick.

Kicking Practices

The ideal practice area is a high, netted enclosure such as an indoor or outdoor cricket net or a golf driving practice net, as this reduces retrieval time and allows the kicker to concentrate on the contact of his foot with the ball. This type of skills practice is invaluable to the kicker — any American grid-iron follower will have noticed that all the kickers in a grid-iron game are practising into a kicking net until called on to the field.

The routine of the correct strike is vital to the kicker. Making kick after kick, of all the different varieties, and practising the spot, line and follow-through of each kick is essential. Timing of the leg swing, the strike of the ball and the follow-through likewise comes with practice, and building up the strength of legs is also vital. Weight training and extensive flexibility exercises should be programmed for regular kickers. Strength and flexibility of the legs, from the hips down, will ensure a longer kick, and practice will add accuracy to length.

In today's game, a good kicker, both short and long, is a must for any team. We practise attacking with the ball, defence, scrummaging and all the other skills. Why do most coaches and kickers think that all the kicker has to do is pick up the ball and kick it? Kicking is a vital skill and should be practised like any other.

Kick and Catch

In a grid 10 metres wide by 30 metres long, place two kickers with one football. Set the kickers the skills practice of kicking the ball to each other but place the emphasis on accuracy. Using all the types of kick, the kicker attempts to place the ball directly into the catcher's arms without the catcher moving. They start with kicks of about ten metres and move further apart, mastering one type of kick before moving on to the next.

Marks and Gains

This is a very good kicking and catching drill. Working one against one, two against two, or even three against three on the full playing area, each team attempts to drive the other team back with a series of punts or grubber kicks. When a team gains the advantage of being in the position of having a drop goal or a place kick at goal, it can attempt to score 1 point from the drop kick or 2 points from the place kick. If the kicking team gains touch with a bounce behind any of the catchers, it is rewarded with another kick ten metres infield in line with where the ball crossed touch. The team catching the ball can kick back as quickly as possible to attempt to catch the other team by surprise. The team scoring the most points is the winner.

Punting between the Posts

This practice can be very useful in developing accurate kicking. Variation of angle and distance can be achieved by setting up a marker cone in front of the posts, say 15 metres infield, and then moving the cone across.

Punting on the Point

This kicking skill is used in grid-iron football and also by Australian rugby players in particular. Punting with the instep down the length of the ball gives length of kick. Punting on the point of the ball gives height for the bomb or up-and-under. Simply pour the ball down, point first, to the kicking foot and punch the ball upwards, keeping the instep in contact with the point of the ball.

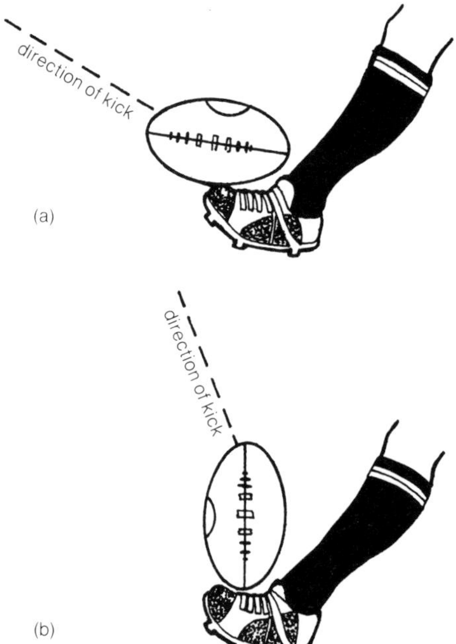

Fig 115   Foot contact in the punt (a) for length of kick (b) for bomb or up-and-under.

This gives a higher, shorter-length kick and is ideal near the opponents' try line. The kicker can practise punting on the point by striking the ball at around thigh-height. The pouring of the ball from the hands is very short indeed and the high contact point gives added height to the kick. Whilst practising punting on the point, the kicker should aim to drop the ball as near to a goal post as possible.

The Grubber Kick

Working two or three players in a group with one football, allow them to grubber kick towards each other in turn, varying the length of kick and practising whilst on the run also. In a grid 37 metres wide by 50 metres long (one quarter of a full pitch) place two sets of marker cones centrally at the ends of the grid as goal posts. Place another two sets of cones centrally, one set down each touchline. The two cones in each set should be 5 metres apart. In a four-against-four grubber practice, the drill is played as touch and play but the object is for the team in possession to gain a position in which to grubber kick through the sets of markers around the grid touch line or between the goal post markers. A team is awarded 1 point for kicking through the touchline cones and 2 points through the goal post markers (no tries are allowed). Practise also in pairs, with one player grub kicking through for his partner to chase, regathering and kicking on the run for his partner.

The Drop Kick

After net kicking, to practise the timing, leg swing and follow-through, another good practice is to drop kick at the goal posts area as if attempting to score a drop goal. Work on various angles and varying lengths of kick. Set up attacking ploys and bring in your drop kicker to try for the one point score. Also practise drop kicking downfield from under the goal posts and from the centre of the 22-metre line.

The Place Kick

Whilst most of the team should be encouraged to practise the various punts, the grubber kick and the drop kick, the place kick is very much a specialist skill. Most teams have no more than two or three players who possess the place-kicking ability required. Concentration, power, timing and above all the correct attitude are essential to the regular place kicker. The top-class place kicker is one who wants the job and kicks regularly for the team; having an extra or reserve place kicker in the side is a very big bonus. It is vital that the team's kickers practise as many times per week as possible on this skill. Net practice is ideal, but there are also a couple of exercises which the goal kicker can practise.

Place Kicking down a Line Using a line marking such as a touchline on the full-sized field, place the ball on a sand tee on the line marking. A team mate stands on the same line around 20–30 metres away facing the kicker and the kicker attempts to place kick the ball straight down the line for him to catch on the full. Adjust the catcher either nearer or further away from the kicker once the kicker is placing the ball accurately over the first distance. This exercise enables the kicker to practise straight and accurate kicking. All the team's place kickers could be working on this drill at the same time along the various lines on or around the playing pitch. A similar drill is to have the kickers place the ball on the corner-flag mark and aim to hit the near post.

Kicking at Goal   After sorting out his best run-up and striking point, the kicker should have plenty of practice time to kick for goal, as in a game. The kicker can practise near the posts to build confidence, and then move on to the longer, harder-angled kicks. Remember the golden rules, both in practice and in games: spot, line and follow-through.

Coaching Points

Place Kick
1. Ball teed up on sand.
2. Much care on line of ball to posts.
3. Eyes on striking point.
4. Correct line of run-up and then approach.
5. Correct swing of leg and contact.
6. Correct follow-through, with head down.

Punt
1. Ball held, as for passing, in cradle.
2. Ball poured down from hands to foot.
3. Eyes on ball.
4. Ball struck at contact with full instep.
5. Good, high follow-through with head down.

Spiral Punt
1. Ball held at 45 degrees across body.
2. Ball poured down from hands to foot at 45 degrees.
3. Eyes on ball.
4. Ball struck with kicking foot instep.
5. Kicking foot slices under and across ball on contact.
6. Head kept down, good follow-through.

Punting on the Point
1. Ball held upright in hands
2. Ball poured, still upright, on to kicking foot.

3. Bottom point of ball struck with instep.
4. Eyes on ball, head down.
5. Contact on ball around hip level for height.
6. Good follow-through.

Drop Kick
1. Ball held, as for passing, in cradle.
2. Ball poured down at 45 degrees.
3. Ball struck with kicking foot instep on the half volley, just as ball touches ground.
4. Eyes on ball, head down.
5. Body leaning slightly backwards.
6. Good, high follow-through.

Grubber Kick
1. Ball held, as for passing, in cradle.
2. Ball poured to ground.
3. Ball stabbed into ground with instep of kicking foot.
4. Body leaning over ball to keep it down.
5. Short, stab follow-through.

CATCHING A HIGH BALL

The final individual skill of catching a high ball is one which should be practised by all players. The principles of catching a high ball start with the catcher gaining a position under the ball as quickly as possible, with eyes on the ball, elbows into the body, hands and fingers outspread forming a cradle for the ball to drop in. As the ball falls towards the catcher he keeps his eyes on the ball and maintains his hand and arm position. On the moment of contact the hands and forearms envelop the ball into the cradle and the ball is cushioned against the chest. The catcher then turns his shoulder towards any supporting or chasing opponent, thus maintaining a good control of the ball.

Fig 116   The player has his eyes on the ball and his arms in the correct position.

Fig 117   The ball is cushioned to the upper chest.

Catching Practice

A good time to practise the catch is when practising the punt with two people, one kicking, the other catching. Working in a grid 10 metres wide by 20 metres long, work a dual practice of the bomb and the catch. One player kicks up the bomb and the catcher completes the catch then kicks back to his partner and so on. The skill of catching a high ball can also be practised in 'marks and gains' (*see* page 72).

Coaching Points

1. Position under ball quickly.
2. Eyes on ball.
3. Correct position of hands and arms.
4. Control of ball on contact.
5. Cradle shape of hands and arms maintained.
6. Ball cushioned to chest on contact.
7. Shoulder turned towards opposition chasers.

3 Team Skills in Attack and Defence

The top teams operate on a theory of the game being played in two phases — attack and defence — and in this chapter we will look at team skills in both phases.

ATTACK

Kick-Off Positions

The whole of your half of the field should be covered when receiving the ball from the kick-off, but the vital areas are the dead-ball line, both touchlines and the immediate line 10 metres from half-way. If the team has several excellent high-ball catchers, they should be placed in the most used catching areas. If the team has some good ground fielders of the ball, players who excel in picking up a rolling or moving ball, they should be positioned in a station where a rolling ball might be expected. Having decided the correct formula of catchers and ground fielders, the other positions at the kick-off pick themselves.

A suggested receiving line-up is 4, 3, 3, 3:

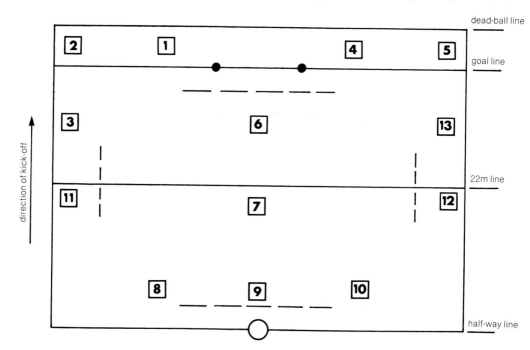

Fig 118   Suggested receiving positions at the kick-off.

four players guarding the dead-ball line, three players covering the line midway across your own 22-metre area, three players covering the line just outside your 22-metre area, and three players guarding against the short kick-off just behind the 10-metre line. This system, or any similar one, allows the team to cover not only the width of the field but also a line down the centre of the playing area.

The perimeter receivers, down both touchlines and across the dead-ball line, should stand just a few centimetres inside the field of play, so that they are aware of where their lines are. Sometimes a receiving player will stand too far infield and the ball may bounce behind them and go into touch or over the dead-ball line. It is much easier to run forward to catch or pick up a ball landing in front than to retrieve a ball going away.

The three receivers covering the short 10-metre kick-off must stand back about a metres from that line. This allows them to gauge the length of the kick-off and ensure that the ball has travelled the required 10 metres forward. The two remaining players cover the midfield kick-off. All players must be prepared to support the team mate who gains possession from the kick-off.

Gaining Possession from Kick-Off

Centrefield Attack

Most teams operate a game plan which includes bringing the ball into centrefield as early in the six tackles as possible. This ploy allows them the option of attacking to left and/or right. A team working close to a touchline limits its attack options. A receiver on the dead-ball line can move forward and

bring in support on either right or left, or can link up with the player in the middle of the 22-metre area. Many well-organised teams like Wigan have a strong running forward as one of their dead-ball-line receivers, either to catch the ball himself and charge downfield or immediately to support a team mate gaining possession.

Bringing the ball into centrefield also gives scope to the kicker. A game plan may involve a kick downfield or to touch early in the series of six tackles. If the kick is downfield, the kicker has the choice of kicking into the right or left sector. If to touch, he can weigh up which touchline is least covered and place his punt or grubber kick to that line.

Touchline Attack

Although a team working the touchline is limited in its attack, there are some factors in its favour. Using a narrow side or blind side can sometimes be advantageous. The touchline nearest your play is always easier to hit with an accurate kick. The midfield bomb or up-and-under infield from a touchline can also be used to great advantage. Another touchline ploy is feigning to pass the ball to the open side, then switching back to overload the short or blind side.

Clearing the Goal Line

Whichever game plan a team employs, there will be periods when it is necessary to clear the ball away from the goal or try-line area. Remembering that a team has only five tackles in which to make ground before a handover or kick, it is essential that the ball is controlled from each play the ball or ruck. The most common ploy to clear the line is using the forwards to gain yardage upfield before bringing in the kicker.

Team Skills in Attack and Defence

The Dummy Half

The dummy halfback is the key figure at each play the ball and he should direct every attack. As he approaches his dummy half station he must decide which way the attack will go, so that he knows which way he will pass before he receives the ball. Before he takes up his position he will look for any weak areas in the opposition's defensive line-up. He may decide to run himself instead of passing, or he may see the opposition fullback out of position and kick directly from dummy half.

It is vital to ensure that the first or second runner receiving the pass from the dummy halfback crosses at speed the line of advantage (the line through the ball being played). This simple ploy guarantees that the team gains yardage at each play the ball and gives a roll-on effect to the forward drives. A quick, accurate play the ball from each ruck to a forward coming on the burst from just behind square, invariably makes crucial yards. If the dummy half passes the ball too far back from the line of advantage, the chances are that the forward will be tackled on or behind the line of advantage and ground will be lost. The dummy half must be a thinker and a very, very skilful player indeed.

Driving Forward

The receiving forward must take the football into the opposition hard, straight and at speed. He must run at the gap between two tacklers and hit the line of defence straight on. Running across the defensive line will mean being picked off and knocked back and over. The forward must concentrate on holding on to the ball, even though confronted by some hard tacklers.

If the dummy half decides to run the ball

out himself, he should firstly gain full control of the ball from the ground, then shoot away at top speed, again aiming for a gap between two defenders, or for a gap he has spotted earlier.

Supporting the Drive Forward

Whoever drives the ball into the opposition defence, he must be supported by his team mates in order to produce a clear attacking break. Much emphasis should be placed on practising team support play.

Communication, the act of conveying a support position to a team mate, is essential. Any player in the vicinity of the ball on attack should call early to the runner and take up a simple and intelligent support position. It is bad play to call for the ball when in a bad position, either too far away from the runner or separated from the runner by defenders. At other times, the supporting team mate may overrun the ball carrier by incorrectly timing his supporting run.

In all support play it is worth remembering one of the oldest adages in Rugby League: 'In a game you may support ninety-nine times and not receive a pass, but on the one hundreth time it may come and you may score the winner.'

Attacking Wide

When clearing the try-line area, safety demands that forwards hold on to the ball in the tackle. The thought of passing the ball wide near the try line may cause a lot of concern to some coaches. But if the opposition defence is weaker out wide and stronger around the ruck of the play the ball sector, why not attack them where they are weak? This is where passing practice is so important. Good teams and good individual layers have the confidence to do this. The unexpected works wonders — what team expects to be attacked out wide by a team bringing the football away from their own try line?

Controlled football with natural flair and the use of surprise adds up to the successful side. If safety is the only factor in your game, you may be the most boring team playing Rugby League. Flair is a match winner — use it.

Attacking from the Play The Ball

We have already stressed the pivotal role of the dummy halfback and receiving forward at the play the ball. We will now look in more detail at tactical attacking ploys in this situation.

Wide Passing Attack

Depth and width of attack are very important when attacking inside the

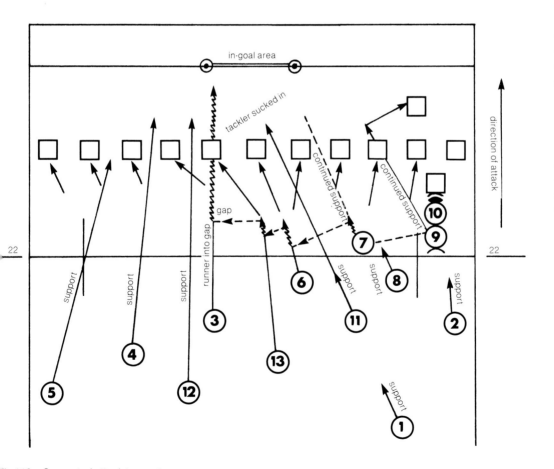

Fig 119 Suggested attack to create gap.

opposition '22' area and elsewhere, and various types of pass and surprise set piece can be introduced in moving the ball wide.

Variation, surprise, speed and accuracy are the key factors. Simply to pass the ball wide and deep along an attacking line will not always burst through an opponent's defence. The aim is to create a gap in the defence, and this may be done in a number of ways.

1.   The different types of pass described in Chapter 2 may create an overlap for the centre or wingman.

2.   An attacking runner can straighten u into the defence, hoping to suck in a tackle and bring him out of his ideal defensiv position. This creates a gap in the defensiv line for a running player to slice through.

3.   A drop-off pass can cause havoc in th defence once the ball has been moved wide The defence is caught running across an back towards its own try line, and the bal carrying attacker drops off his team mat into the gap created by the changing angl of attack.

4.   A two-line attack is a simple bu effective method of breaking a defence. ■

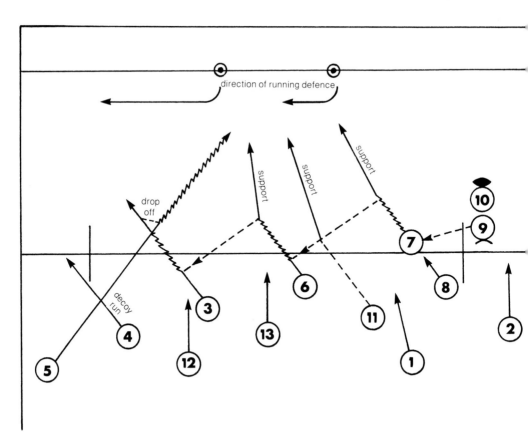

Fig 120   *Changing the angle of attack by bringing in the winger with a drop-off pass.*

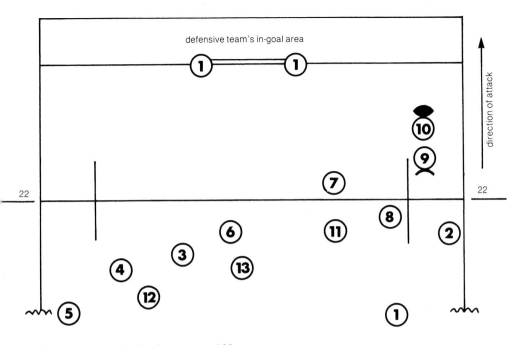

ig 121   Suggested attacking line in opponents' 22.

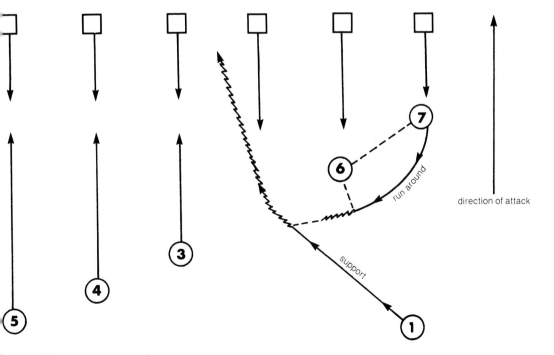

Fig 122   Run around pass creating a gap.

depends on hitting the defence wide and using a second line of attackers behind the handlers as pure support players, as shock troops via a miss out or face pass, or to continue an attack quickly if any of the first-line attackers are tackled.

5. The run around pass can be used to great effect when moving the ball wide, creating a gap either for the receiver himself or for his supporting team mate.

Once the intended break through the defence is achieved, support play is vital. The man making the break must have the support of his team mates in continuing the break and maintaining the continuity of the attack. Many times a superb break filters away because of lack of support. The fullback should be encouraged to come into the attack as much as possible to provide extra options. Similarly wingers' pace should be used in midfield and elsewhere as a shock tactic during attack.

Attacking Close to the Ruck

When attacking from the play the ball close to the ruck, the team's straight runners should obviously be concentrated near the play the ball area. The dummy half is again the key figure: when running the football his scoot away should be sharp, fast and into the gap between tacklers; when passing to running team mates his weighting must be accurate and his timing perfect. The object of the driving runner should be to make as much yardage forward as possible and always to cross the advantage line. The normal rule for driving forwards is to hit the football up into the opponents' defence as hard and straight as possible and to add support in numbers each time the ball is driven in. There are several possible

variations of the attack close to the play the ball.

1. The first receiver can be sent in. This the most common attack.
2. The dummy half can scoot awa himself. This method of attack can gain lot of yardage and often results in a clear brea for the dummy half.
3. The use of decoy runners can b advantageous. One simple move to gai ground from the play the ball is the mis pass — the dummy half misses the firs decoy runner and hits a second runne coming in just behind.
4. The crisscross move from the play th ball is another good variation. Starting with cross one set piece, building to a cross tw and then bringing in a cross three, this ur complicated ploy works well in any sector c the field. The cross one simply brings th runner across the back of the dummy half t change the angle of attack. The cross tw continues the variation from the next pla the ball. The cross three is used near th opponents' try line in an attempt to burs over and score.
5. The turn-back or decoy drop-off move i another defence-splitting manoeuvre from the play the ball. The dummy half dummies t a cross one decoy runner, scoots awa square to the advantage line and drops off runner down the side of the ruck. The defenc covers the decoy, chases the dummy ha and leaves a gap at the side of the play th ball. Another drop-off pass move is for the firs receiver to run directly back towards th dummy half on taking his pass and bring in a angled runner through the gap he has create by his change of direction.

Many simple moves from close to the ruc can be plotted during a game, and consider ing that there are vastly more play the ball

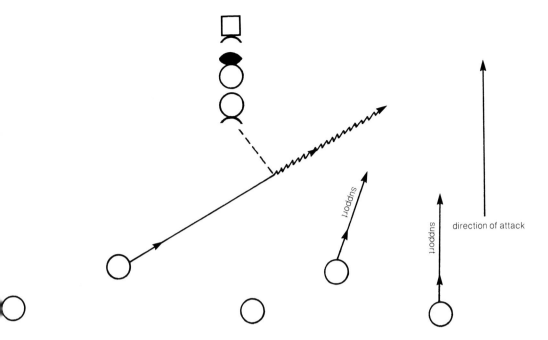

Fig 123   Criss-cross moves at play the ball: cross 1.

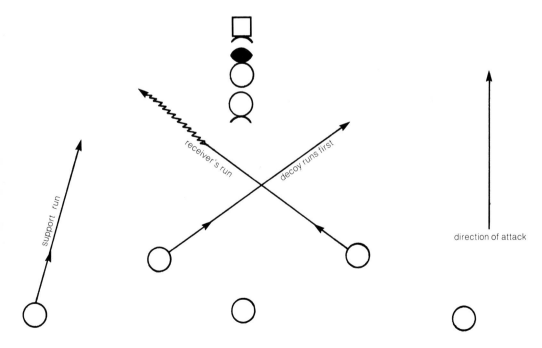

Fig 124   Cross two.

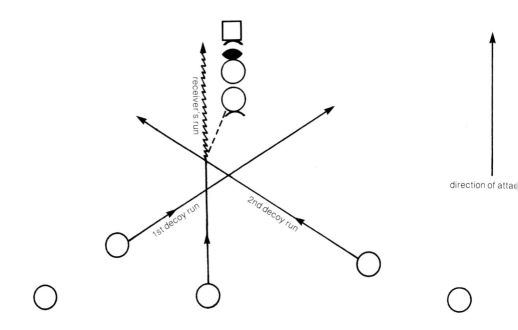

direction of attack

Fig 125   Cross three.

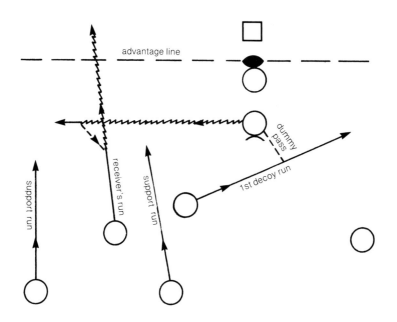

advantage line

dummy pass

direction of attack

Fig 126   Cross one, drop-off move.

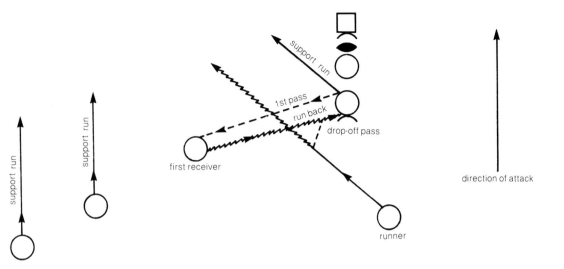

Fig 127   First receiver drop-off.

in a game than any other skills it is only common sense to concentrate on these attacking opportunities.

Attacking from a Scrummage

Attacking by the backs is advised whenever the team wins the ball in a scrum. The modern-day laws of the game demand that both sets of backs shall be at least 5 metres behind their respective loose forwards and this gives the side winning the scrummage a tremendous opportunity to attack at speed using their halfbacks, three-quarters and fullback. Scrums can be set down by the referee anywhere within 10 metres from the touchlines and 5 metres from the try lines. Imagine the scope given to the team winning the ball if, for instance, it wins the scrum 10 metres in from touch, with 65 metres in width to play in. There are again several variations of the scrum attack.

1.   Bringing in the fullback to make the extra man in attack is a well-used move. The fullback can come up into the back line in whatever position he decides, directly off the stand-off half or scrum half, between stand-off and first centre, between the centres, or between outside centre and winger. Operating a run around pass between first centre and stand-off half, the stand-off passes to the centre, runs around him, takes the return run around pass and hits the fullback coming hard and straight into the gap between the two defending centre three-quarters. The attacking fullback is then challenged by his opposite number, the defending fullback, and good support play should follow. A similar move from the scrum is for the stand-off, No.6, to miss out the first centre, No.3, and hit the full back, No.1, coming hard on to the pass, between the defending centres.

2.   Another good move is the centre switch, where the stand-off, No.6, decoy runs across the back of the scrum and the blind-side centre angles back and takes the pass of the scrum half, No.7.

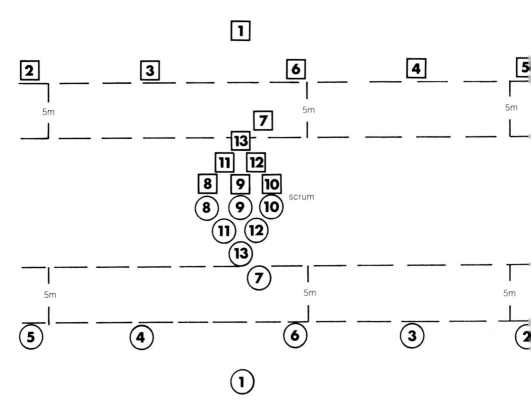

Fig 128   On-side positions at scrum.

3. A most effective stand-off/centre move from a scrummage is the outside centre drop-off. The stand-off half, No. 6, and the first centre, No.4, run parallel to each other across field. The outside centre, No.3, times his run to take a drop-off pass from the stand-off and hits the gap created by the cross-field run.

4. Wingmen too should be used on attack from a scrum. In a scrum down 10 metres from the right-hand touchline, the right winger should be brought around behind the stand-off and first centre to take a short, weighted pass, as it were on the loop, from the first centre. Sending a winger with pace into midfield causes problems for any defence. A very effective and well-used ploy is to bring in the loose forward, No.13, to spring a move directly from the base of the scrum. This particular move is codenamed 'Featherstone' after its place of origin. Winning a scrum near the opponents' try line, the scrum half stoops to pick up the ball behind the scrum, leaves the ball at the loose forward's feet and runs decoy without the ball to the blind side of the scrum. The loose forward picks up the ball and runs directly at the opponents' stand-off half on the open side, taking his own stand-off with him as support. Invariably this leads to a breakdown in defence and, more often than not, a try to the attacking team.

As with all moves and set pieces it is absolutely essential to practise them during training/coaching sessions, until the team can do them blindfold. Various ball handlers and runners should be intermixed, so that

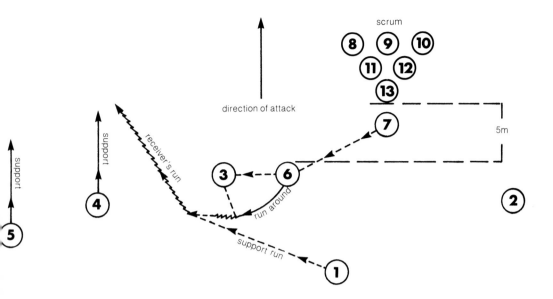

Fig 129   Fullback attacking from a run around at scrum.

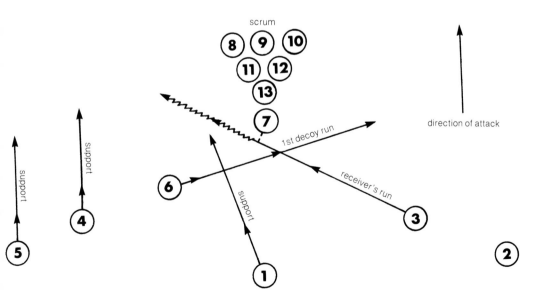

Fig 130   Attacking from a scrum − centre switch move.

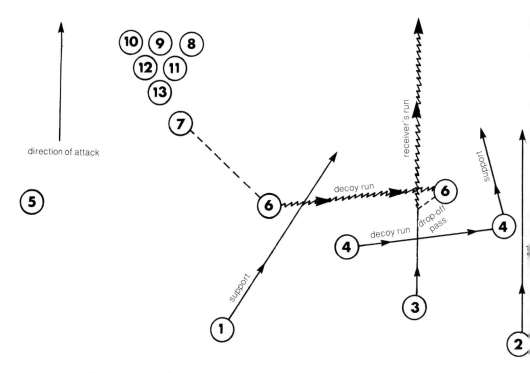

Fig 131   Outside centre drop-off move.

any player can take up any part of the move. Some teams rely on only one ball handler. This is a mistake — what would happen if he received an injury early in the game? Imagine the complete breakdown of a game plan if the key player is missing.

Attacking from a Kick Through

By Your Own Team

The two most common kicks to gain ground or regain possession are the tactical chip punt and the grubber kick through the opposition defence. Both can be devastating when performed correctly. The tactical chip punt is kicked diagonally in behind the advancing defensive line; the grubber kick, along the ground into the opposition's in-goal area, is very difficult indeed for the defence to control. We will return to the tactical use of these kicks in Chapter 4.

By the Opposition

Most teams use the punt kick to gain ground on or around the fifth tackle. Most teams will kick straight downfield or angle the kick towards a touchline and chase. The good positional play of the fullback and wingers is then very important.

The fullback is required to concentrate on his field position, usually behind the line of the ball but also being prepared to cover the touchlines should the opposition kick for the side line. He must read the opposition's kicking game. It is prudent for him to know his opponents, and which player kicks for them, when they kick and how far. If the opposing team kicks directly at him, he must have the skill and confidence to catch the ball on the full and avoid letting it bounce in front of him. By reading the game just prior to the kick, he will be aware of the concentration of opposition chasers. His first priority is to catch and control the ball, and his second is to attack by running hard and strong at the opposition's weak point. If the fullback is an elusive, skilful runner, he may decide to take on a chasing forward and attempt to set up an attack by beating the chaser who is first up with a side step, a swerve or by sheer pace. Or he may decide to run to the area of his own forwards, giving the team the option of various forward plays from his play the ball.

Wingmen too must play a large part in attacking from the opponents' kick through. Good wingers will also read the game and chase back to support their fullback in his attempt to attack from catching the kick through. If the opposition kick to a touchline, the winger fields the ball. It would be foolish for him to try to run the ball close to the touchline because of the danger of being tackled into touch on the team's first tackle. Wingers should run the ball infield, to leave attacking options both sides of the play the ball.

Should the opposing team kick downfield parallel to the touch line and the ball be fielded clearly by the fullback, a good ploy is for him to run the ball wide across field and link up, in attack, with the furthest centre and winger, who would both chase back in their own sector of the field to support him. This passage of play changes the area of attack quickly and normally offers the fullback, far centre and winger the opportunity

to run into space. Not all kicking and chasing teams cover the full width of the field — most kick-chasers cover only the narrow area around their kicker and the outer areas are vulnerable to a fast, wide attack.

Attacking from a Hand-Over

In Rugby League the hand-over occurs when a team is held for six consecutive tackles. They must then hand over the football to their opponents, who bring it back into play with a normal play the ball. The hand-over must be completed quickly and fairly by the tackled team and this first play the ball immediately on hand-over gives great advantage to the team regaining possession and a great opportunity to spring an attack. More often than not the defending side does not have the time to set up its defence correctly.

Options at this stage of the game are many and varied. A defender may be struggling to get back into defensive line, so an attack may be aimed at him. If the opponents' forwards are held on the last tackle using short support play, at hand-over most of them will be around the area of the ball, so three passes out from the play the ball may attack an almost undefended sector. A quick, accurate play the ball with good support and awareness of the defence's weak point will assist a team in breaking the defensive line. Simply driving the ball in will give the defence time to reassert itself.

Attacking from a Tap Kick

After a successful penalty kick to touch, the game is restarted with a tap kick 10 metres infield, in line with where the ball crossed the touchline. The full defensive team must retire at least 10 metres back from the point of the tap kick, unless the ball has crossed the touchline within 10 metres of the defenders' try line in which case the defending team would only retire to that line.

The tap kick is the usual starting point for many complicated, almost exotic, moves and set pieces. Attacking walls are constructed by players, criss-cross moves abound, decoy runners appear in almost every direction. Up until a few seasons ago, a flying wedge move was allowed where all the attacking forwards would form a loose scrummage behind the tap kicker and attempt to push him over his opponents' try line. This flying wedge is now outlawed because of obstruction against the defence. An uncomplicated move from the tap kick is in order, but if a team possesses the ability to work these more complicated set pieces, it should practise them in training and use them.

Attacking from a tap kick 10 metres from a touchline limits a team's options slightly, but also gives opportunities. The defensive team has on the one hand only a very short blind side to cover but on the other a very wide open side of 65 metres to defend.

On the Blind Side

If an attack is to be aimed at the blind side, the usual ploy is to appear to be attacking open side and then switch back to the blind side quickly. Most professional coaches prefer moving the ball into centrefield from a 10-metre tap kick because this gives the attacking team the option of attacking left or right of the ensuing play the ball or even through the guts of the ruck. Keeping the ball down the blind side tends to make a forward battle of the game.

One ploy is to set up a wall of two, three or more attacking players facing their own goal line with backs towards the opposition

defence. The wall is designed to hide the ball from the defence and allow a surprise runner burst through at the defence, and the variations on it are many. In the blind side overload (see Fig. 132), the intention is to use an overload of runners to punch a hole in the defence. Another option is two drives infield and switch to remove a blind side defender then hit back blind with a powerful runner.

On the Open Side

A good open side set piece involves the winger, with the forwards playing a major role and with two run around and drop-off passes. At the third play the ball the run around passer acts as decoy runner and the winger slices in on the angle to take the pass close to the pivot and burst through the defence.

A set pattern of three tramline moves, involving hitting both open and blind side areas is another method of breaking a defence. These patterns should be used one after another. They are set up exactly the same each time but produce a varied end result.

The normal defensive position against a tap kick is spread out across the open side of the field from the tap kicker and covering about 12–15 metres. To attack wide from the tap kick and send in powerful forward runners against the opposition three-quarters, the use of two or three quick, long and deep passes immediately from the tap kick can be a devastating move. These passes clear the ball very quickly away from the opposition's forward defensive screen, allowing the attacking team to overload the weaker tackling area of the other team's backs.

Another wide attacking move from the tap kick is to use the three-quarters to move

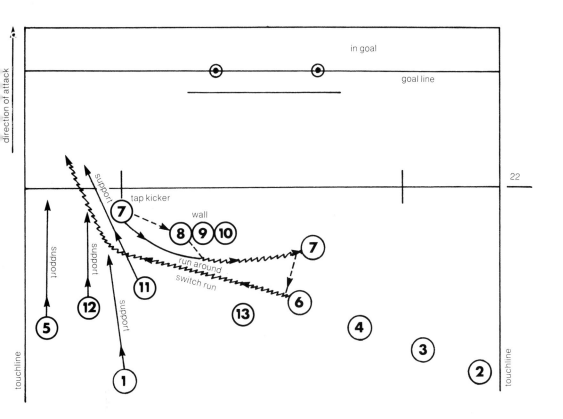

the ball across the field with a quick succession of passes and short runs to the line of advantage. This aims to catch the opponents' defence on the change. At the tap kick the attacking line of passing backs are opposed by the opponents' forwards. After moving the ball wide and sending in a driving forward, the opponents' forwards and backs are caught in the wrong defensive position – the attacking forwards are running into the defending backs and the defending forwards are left in a non-tackling position. Phase two of this attack is to switch play back to the three-quarters immediately from the first play the ball. Should the opposing forward defensive screen not change position, the attacking side's faster, more elusive backs will be confronting the opposing forwards, and will have the

Fig 132   Attacking from a tap kick – wall move with blind side overload.

support of fullback, loose forward and second-row forward.

Whichever moves are used from a tap kick, they must be practised endlessly. Set pieces may be changed to suit the opposition, but always keep the moves to a sound basic skills level at first. Once a team has mastered the basic principles, then, and only then, can it progress to the more complicated set pieces. Organising the various ball handlers, decoy runners and receiving runners is an important part of the game plan, and the responsibility of carrying out the game plan should only be given to the players who can do the job well. The game plan should take account of players' individual abilities, but in the ideal team each player should be interchangeable. This again emphasises the importance of a good skills-orientated training programme.

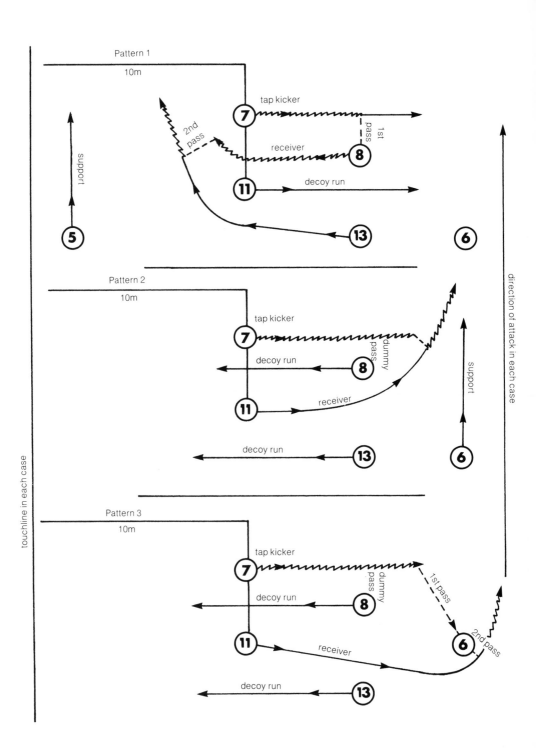

Fig 133   Tramline patterns for the attack.

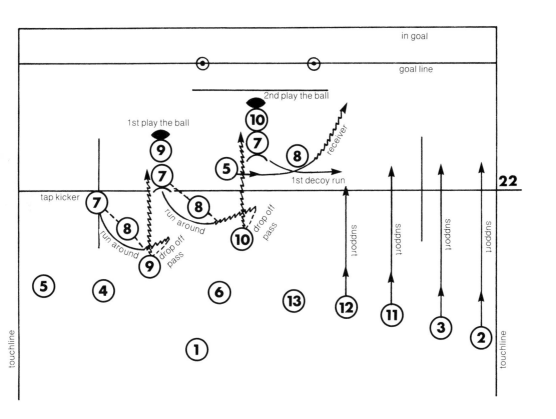

Fig 134 Bringing in the winger.

DEFENCE

Kick-Off Positions

Remembering that the attacking team is always the side in possession of the football, no matter where they are in the field of play, the team taking the kick-off is in effect immediately on the defensive. The game plan starts with how much pressure the team kicking off can inflict on the attacking team and determines which type of kick-off position is required.

Containment from a Long Kick-Off

To contain the opposition in a corner section of the field near their own try line, the suggested line up would be to position both wingmen, No.2 and No.5, just inside the kicker, No.7. It is vital to have fast chasers covering the midfield area, thus stopping the catching team moving the ball to the open side. A team's wingers are usually fast runners and both would sprint after the kick-off and cover the line of the facing left-hand goal post. The faster forwards, Nos. 11, 12 and 13, would cover the central area

93

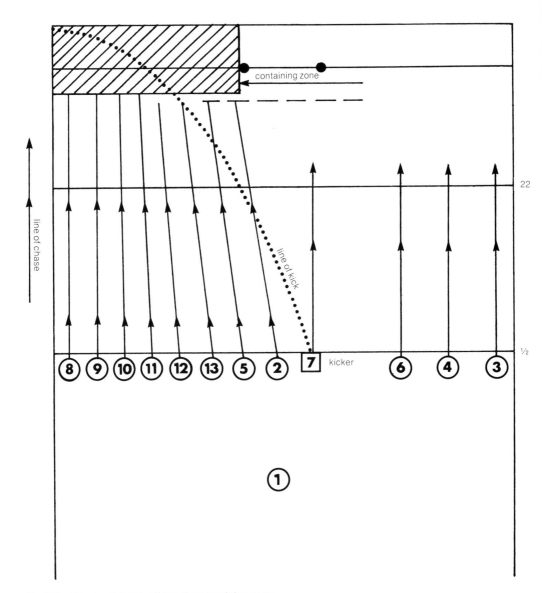

Fig 135   Chasing the kick-off into the containing zone.

between the fast wingers and the slower players, Nos.8, 9 and 10, who would cover the touchline. The fast wingers form a leading point of an arch, the back rowers the centre of the arch and the front row the tail of the arch. The containment zone can be placed anywhere by simply adjusting the faster runners into the leading arch positions.

Short Kick-Off

A variation at the kick-off is the short kick, but the kicking side must take great care and practise long and hard before this very skilful kick is attempted. The kicker places a short, high kick-off from the centre spot, aiming at the unguarded area in front of

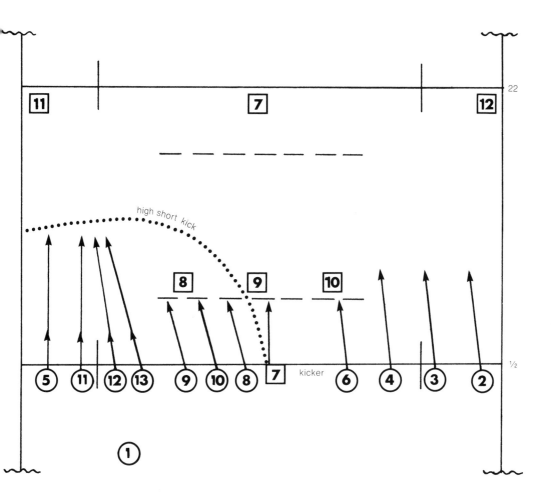

Fig 136   Short kick-off to regain possession.

catcher No.11 and behind catcher No.8. The football should be kicked about 15 metres downfield and land around 10 metres from touch, ensuring that the ball crosses the line 10 metres from half way in the opponents' half. The height of the kick is crucial – a good, accurate, high kick allows the chasers, Nos. 5, 11, 12 and 13, time to get under the ball as it drops to the ground. This type of short kick-off is aimed to regain possession, not to contain.

Defending at the Play The Ball

One-Line Defence

The basic principle of a one-line defence is that all the team except the fullback and the play the ball marker spread in one line across the field, aiming to defend directly opposite the attackers they are marking. In theory, the defending side has the advantage at each play the ball. The attacking side has one man as ball player with a dummy half behind him and the fullback usually in a deep position, while the defence has one man at marker and the fullback deep. Good odds — eleven against ten.

When the ball has cleared the ruck of the play the ball, that is when the ball has left the playing foot of the play the ball player, the defending team can move in to tackle the attacking team. Moving-in in ones and twos creates gaps in the defence. The line must move up together initially and communicate with one another verbally. Encouraging each other and moving in together helps to maintain the line. Some psychological phrases help too. For instance, name-dropping —

e.g. 'I'll take Smith this time' — may cause the attacker to lose concentration for a second.

Coaching Points

1. Look to the referee at each set up of play the ball. He will give you the on-side 5-metre mark. Do not be caught off-side. Do not give away off-side penalties.

2. Move in together, in one line, when defending. Do not allow any team member to rush in and create a gap on each side of him. Communicate verbally with each other at all times on defence and name-drop the opposition at every opportunity.

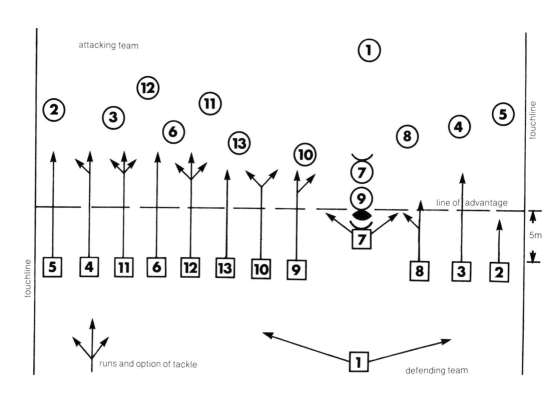

Fig 137 One-line defence at play the ball.

3. Tackle with the utmost determination at all times. Avoid tackling high — first man in goes low to block the legs, second man blocks and traps the ball.

4. After each tackle the defensive line retreats together, back-pedalling and facing the opposition, to the line of on-side mark given by the referee. Communicate and encourage each other at all times.

Shuffle Defence

Whenever the attacking team are passing laterally, the one-line defence is a sound tactic. But suppose the attacking ball carrier straightens up directly at his defending head-on opponent and just before the tackle passes to a support player running into the gap very close to the ball carrier. This is the time to operate the 'shuffle' defence system. The ball carrier, who straightens the attack by running directly at the try line, must be challenged quickly by a defender. The defenders to the tackler's right and left leave their opposite attacker and cover the gaps to each side of the ball carrier. Every defender across the defensive line angles in one attacking place. This shuffle eliminates the chances of a break from a short support pass.

Coaching Points

1. Maintain on-side position.
2. Each man angles in towards tackle area one place on both sides, in one line.
3. Tackle strongly.
4. After tackle retreat at same angle in one line to referee's mark.
5. Communicate and encourage.

Umbrella Defence

This system too can be used against a wide attacking opposition. It is widely used in Australian Rugby League and is very effective either at nullifying wide attacks or at controlling the attackers' area by using an umbrella of space around the play the ball ruck.

Coaching Points

1. Keep on-side.
2. Outside men sprint up into the attacking line quickly, taking the rest of their defensive line up with them to get in amongst the attackers once the ball has cleared the ruck of the play the ball.
3. Retreat quickly to an on-side position after each tackle.
4. Tackle with determination and strength — good defence wins games.
5. The centre of the umbrella will absorb most of the tackles, but be prepared to defend just as strongly on either outside point of the umbrella.
6. Communicate.

Ruck Area Defence

Without an organised ruck area defence a team can be very vulnerable in that sector. A suggested defence around the play the ball uses either two tight defenders or one blocker — the tight defenders cover each side of the ruck; the blocker is used to defend the area 5 metres away from, and directly behind, the play the ball. The presence of a fullback in the one-line defence system gives in effect two defensive lines: the first is the wing-to-wing front defence, the second is the fullback. Against a good kicking opposition or a team that possesses fast three-quarters, a defence may need three lines of defensive players, with a player, called a 'sweeper' or 'bobby', between the front line and the full back. The bobby's job is to mop up any short

97

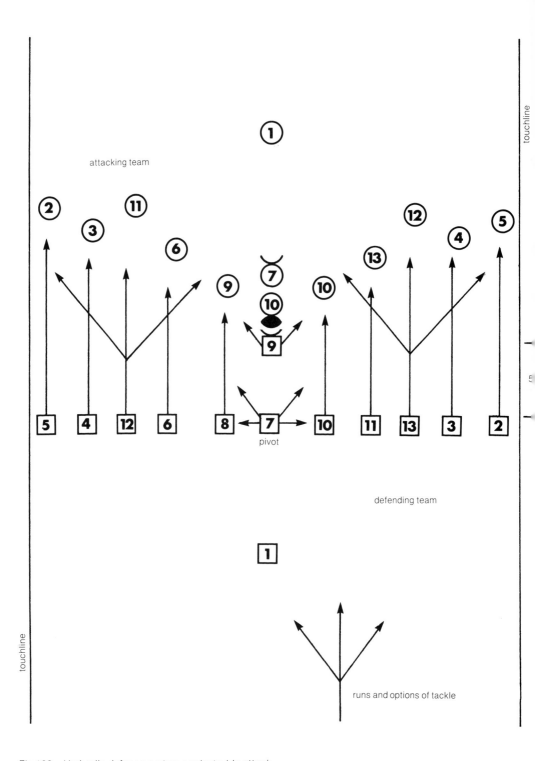

Fig 138   Umbrella defence system against wide attack.

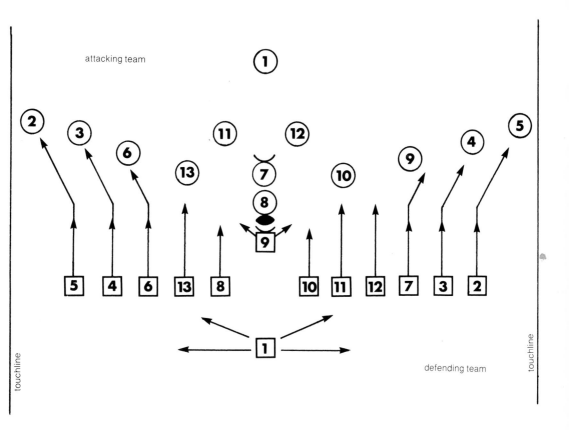

Fig 139   Umbrella defence system to control at ruck.

kick put through the front defensive line, or to cover across behind the front defence and snuff out any break that may occur. He can also assist the fullback and support him quickly should the attackers kick deep.

Coaching Points

1.   Attempt to force the close-in runners back over the line of advantage with a strong challenge every tackle.
2.   Do not stray off-side.
3.   Communicate and name-drop, encourage and assist.

Defending at a Scrummage

In normal circumstances the backs will control the defence at a scrum, as at least half the pack of forwards will be entangled in the just-completed scrummage. The laws of the game demand that at a scrummage both sets of backs shall retire at least 5 metres behind their own scrummaging loose forward, except the scrum half of each side who must be behind his own loose forward when the ball emerges.

   The general defensive tasks of the forwards from a scrum have been described in Chapter 2. The defending team should work on the principle of each man covering his immediate opponent, and defenders should challenge attackers quickly and preferably on the attackers' side of the scrum advantage line. If the attacking scrum half runs the football from the scrum and attacks the blind side, the defending loose forward is the man to tackle him. The loose forward's first priority on breaking from the scrum having lost the ball is to check blind side.

Should the attacking stand-off decide to run the ball, the defending stand-off is responsible for the tackle, and to prevent the attacking team passing wide he should attempt to channel his opponent back towards the just-completed scrum and into the defensive path of his own fast-breaking loose forward and open-side second rower. He achieves this by standing just outside his opponent, apparently leaving a gap in the defence down the open side of the scrum.

Should the attacking team bring its fullback into the attack, the defending fullback covers his opposite number. Centres mark centres and wingers cover wingers.

If the attackers move the ball wide from a scrum, the defending scrum half should cover across the back of his advancing three-quarters and should be supported in his covering run by his loose forward and both second rowers. The fullback covers his opposite number and the blind-side winger covers the fullback position.

Defending against a Kick Through

The Six Tackles

The attacking side can kick the ball at any time they are in possession from the first to the last tackle. Defence against this kick through is very important and being aware of the number of tackles made against the opposition is vital. Most teams hold back their kicks until late in the series of six tackles. If your defensive plan includes a sweeper or bobby, he is responsible for covering midfield chips. On the fourth and fifth tackles of the attacking team a good defence against the kick is to have the bobby in a midfield sweeping role, the two defending wingers covering the kick to touch and the fullback covering the long downfield kick.

Acting Bobby

In this defence against the kick through, two fast-running and nimble players take up defensive positions, one each side of the play the ball ruck. If the attack passes the ball to its left, the acting bobby on the left of the ruck drops out of the first defensive line and drifts into the bobby position behind his advancing defence. If the attack then kicks the ball whilst moving to its left, the acting bobby covers it. If the attack moves the ball to its right, the acting bobby on the right of the defence covers in the same way. If the attacking team is tackled with no break or kick, the acting bobby returns quickly to his original defensive position. The ideal players to take the acting bobby role are the stand-off half and scrum half.

Weather Conditions

Weather conditions may call for variations in the defensive plans against the kick through. If playing against a strong downfield wind, it is advisable for the fullback to lie very deep to cover the wind-assisted kick through; if with a strong wind, he could stand much nearer to his first line defence. In rainy, wet conditions much care must be taken when regaining possession after a kick through. The ball may well shoot

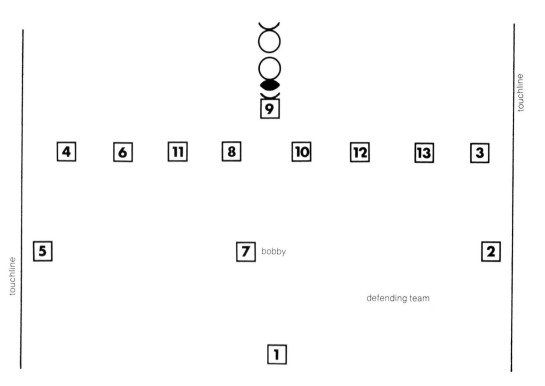

Fig 140   Defence against the kick through — line on 4th and 5th tackle.

forward on bouncing because of the sodden ground, so the ball should be taken on the full, before it bounces. It is also imperative that the whole defending team chases back to support the fielder of the kick through.

Defending at a Hand-Over

Quick thinking and quick actions are called for by the defending team at a hand-over. The defensive line must be organised and in position as soon as possible. The vulnerable areas are around the ruck of the play the ball and the area some 10—15 metres each side of the ruck.

The most effective defender at the ruck is the blocker who covers any break from near the ruck. The back-row forwards, lock and second rowers must attain their correct positions quickly, outside the props, on each side of the ruck. If the hand-over is near a

touchline no forward should stand blind side resting. Standing opposite the attacker and simply counting the attackers each side of the ruck is an easy way to cover any attempted breakthrough.

The fullback can play an important role in organising the defence at a hand-over. He has possibly the best view of any positional weaknesses from his station in the rear, and he should call out clearly to any defender who needs to move to his right or left. Communication in defence, as ever, is crucial.

Defending at a Tap Kick

As we saw earlier, most teams are keen to work some type of planned move at the tap kick. As soon as the tap kick is taken, it is essential that the defensive line moves up in one unbroken line on the attackers. Concentration is required in this vital defensive

101

position and care must be taken not to be out-thought by the attack. Most set piece moves are designed in the hope that the defence will come rushing in. Move in steadily but in a controlled manner, each tackler picking his target in advance and covering the area at each side of the ball carrier. To buy a dummy or hesitate when confronted by a decoy runner can spell disaster.

The defence must check that they are all in line with the touch judge, 10 metres from the point of the tap kick. The touch judge will hold out his flag at shoulder height until all the defenders are in line. Bad concentration can lose a team many yards if caught offside at the tap penalty kick.

UNOPPOSED DRILLS AND OPPOSED PRACTICE

This is a fairly new innovation in our country, taken again from Australian Rugby League, which in turn took it from American grid-iron football. It is simply a series of team attack and defence drills on the full-sized playing field.

Unopposed Drills

Each pattern of play is first broken down and practised without opposition. To start unopposed drills, the coach or a reserve player kicks off from the centre spot, the team gains possession of the ball and works through its pattern of attacking moves in the area of the field that the coach has chosen. Clearing one's own line, working towards and away from the touchline, using the blind side, playing to centrefield, attacking near the opponents' line, bringing in the kicking game — all these aspects are worked on and gradually a game plan is formulated.

Scrums are formed to allow the backs to practise their set pieces, tap kicks are taken from penalties and time is given to practising set moves from these. Play the balls and the ensuing moves from them are worked out and perfected. When the coach has laid out the game plan on attack to his players he may well retire from the field and check out the unopposed game plan from the touchline or some other position, leaving his team in full control of the session.

The defensive game plan is also worked on and emphasis is placed on those areas which may be vulnerable. Defence practice can be worked on either with an inner tube or a football. The coach, or someone delegated by the coach, kicks the ball along the ground, across the front of the line of defence. The defence moves in quickly, in line both sides of the ruck area, and the ball is dropped on by one of the defensive line. As an alternative to the rolling ball, the coach may introduce an inner tube as the moving target to be tackled. The tube is then rolled across the face of the defence, which moves in and tackles the tube, and so on for a series of five tackles.

If required, the unopposed drill may be used to work on defence or attack only, but a final session may include both aspects. If while attacking, the team drops a ball in passing, the coach calls 'Hand-over' and the team quickly sets up its defensive line. When the team brings in its kicking game, the coach calls 'Tackle' or 'Held' where the ball bounces, and the team sets up the defence there. Similarly, after five tackles of the inner tube during defensive practice, the coach reintroduces the ball and kicks downfield for the team to return to the attack. The drill is repeated after the team's kick through or if it drops the ball in passing. When the team is on defence during this drill, it is advisable to use another member of the squad, say one of the substitutes, to act as referee and give the defence a good 5-metre mark from the point of tube roll. This drill allows the practice to be simulated like a game.

Each section of play can be worked on using the various unopposed drills. Each section can be stopped if needed and practised again and again until the coach and team are satisfied that the execution and timing are perfect. This unopposed drill system is not a training run-out. It is introduced as a skills practice or game plan session.

Opposed Practice

Bringing in some opposition puts a little pressure on the practising players. If two teams operate at the club, work one against the other, but avoid tackling during the practice and use the 'grip' method instead. In the grip method, the would-be tackler simply grips the attacker and the attacker stops running, allowing himself a few seconds as if regaining his feet after the tackle. The attack then continues with a play the ball. Both teams will benefit by this opposed type of practice.

If there are fewer opponents than a full team, one particular drill may be practised with an opposition. For instance, the limited opposition may be placed against the forwards around the ruck or set up against the backs, wide out, to give both the pack and the backs that little pressure while practising the attacking or defensive game plan.

4 The Kicking Game

INTRODUCTION

The advent of limited-tackle Rugby League, and the ensuing change in the laws of the game, brought a new lease of life to the kicking skills. Leading the way in the modern game of skilful kickers are the Australian players. The long, raking punts down the field or to touch, the astute, short grubber kicks behind the on-rushing defensive lines, the near-the-line and midfield bombs, the chip and chases over the heads of defenders, general field kicks — these are all worked on religiously by our Australian coaching and playing counterparts. The kicking game in our club and international teams too is gradually taking on its rightful importance as players and their coaching staff are realising the need to produce quality kickers.

Most Australian coaches study the fabulous kicking techniques of Australian Rules kickers. Australian Rules is a game based wholly on kicking and catching, and is centred around both long and short accurate kicking. Australian coaches dissected the Rules kicking styles — even down to the ways the ball is held — and introduced kicks such as the drop punt into their kicking game. The Australians now rely very heavily indeed on their kicking game, and during the past few years they have produced some of the best all-time kickers in the history of the game. Wally Lewis is accurate to a fine degree and uses all the kicks in his vast armoury of attacking talents to put opposing teams under constant pressure. Peter Stirling is another superb kicker whose short kicking is beautifully executed and always a threat to his opponents.

Great Britain too has produced some great kickers — the legendary Jim Sullivan of Wigan, the superb Jimmy Ledgard of Dewsbury and Leigh, and the one and only Alex Murphy, whose exploits as a player were enhanced by a splendid kicking game. Today's kicking experts in Britain do not outclass the Australians, but Deryk Fox of Featherstone Rovers, Joe Lydon of Wigan and Lee Crooks of Leeds spring to mind as top-class kickers.

CLEARING 'DOWN-TOWN'

'Down-town' is the term widely used for a clearing kick downfield. The ball is passed back to the kicker, who hits the ball downfield into space to give his chasers extra time to isolate the receiver and pick him off with a first-time tackle. The perfect down-town will be placed away from the opposing fullback and ideally make him and the other backs turn and run back towards their own try line.

The down-town kicker will have assessed the positions of the opposition before he kicks. If the opposing wingers have dropped back too deep to cover the touchlines, the kicker may decide to line kick, that is aim to gain ground by kicking to touch, with a bounce, in front of the wingers. Alternatively, if they are covering too shallowly, he may aim behind them.

The position of the down-town kicker, on receiving the pass to kick downfield, is

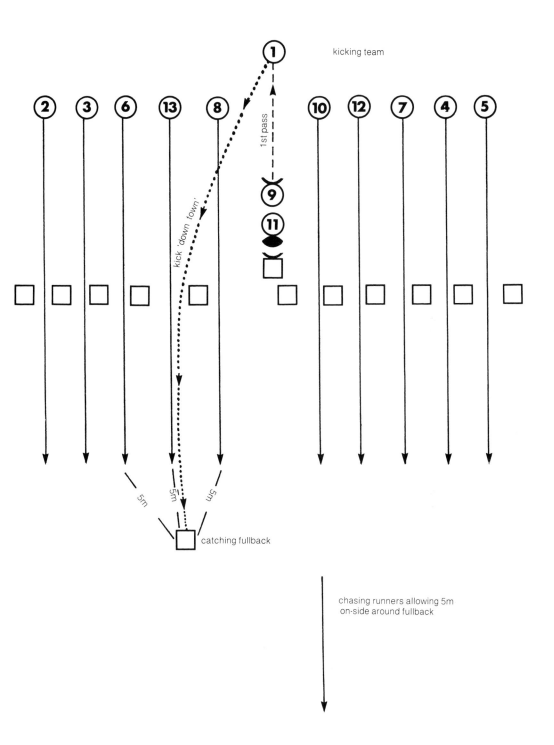

Fig 141   Chasing 'down-town' clearing kick.

important. He must be deep enough not to have his kick charged down by a challenging opponent but not so deep as to affect the pass back to him. To give him that extra second of time, the pass to the kicker should be slightly to his right if he is a right-footed kicker and slightly to his left if left-footed. This enables him to control the pass immediately and transfer the ball quickly and accurately from hands to foot.

The position of the kicker's team mates with regard to off-side is also important. As the down-town clearing kick is normally operated from a pass back after a play the ball, at the kick the majority of the kicker's team are in front of him and technically off-side. The laws relating to this situation are clear enough. If all the kicker's team are in an on-side position at the play the ball — 5 metres behind the line of the ball being played — then they can chase after the kick, but they must allow the ball-retrieving opponent 5 metres until he has run 5 metres in any direction. The chasing team is put on-side once the retriever has fielded the ball and moved 5 metres in any direction from the point of regaining possession.

The chasers are as important as the kick. The down-town is aimed at gaining ground but it is pointless to gain ground by using a long kick, then lose ground by allowing the retriever to run the ball back at the defence. The chasers must sprint downfield, preferably in one line to the width of the field and must effect the first tackle soundly. This gives them the perfect platform to hold the attacking team and exert defensive pressure.

CLOSE-IN AND MIDFIELD BOMBS

The bomb is often used near the opponents' try line in the hope that the defence will drop the ball. If this occurs the advantage is with the chasers, who can regain possession near to their opponents' try line and exert further attacking pressure or even score a try. Remembering that, if he catches the bomb on the full inside his own in-goal area, a defender is allowed to restart the game with a tap kick from the centre of his own 22-metre line, it is prudent to aim to drop the bomb kick just inside the field of play, making the defender attempt the catch just infield from his own try line.

The midfield bomb is aimed into an un-protected area behind the front line of defence but away from the fullback or bobby, and as high as possible to give the attacking chasers time to arrive under the ball as it drops to ground. The intended end product of either bomb kick is to regain possession or score a try.

KICKING THROUGH THE DEFENCE

This is also recommended as a way of regaining possession and mainly concerns the chip punt, face kick and grubber kick.

Chip Punt

The chip punt is a most effective kick, placed either straight or at an angle over the top of the on-rushing defensive line, for the kicker himself or an on-side team mate to chase. The kick must be placed into an un-defended area, not too deep or it may go directly to the bobby or the defending full-back and be ineffective — it is designed to regain possession, not to give the opposition the ball.

Face Kick

Another very successful kick, when near your opponents' try line, is the face kick, or punt across the face of the goal posts. This kick is aimed from about 15 metres to one side of the posts across the field at the far corner flag. It usually catches the far defending centre and winger unawares and often leads to a try.

Grubber Kick

One of the most favoured kicks close to the opponents' line is the grubber into the in-goal area. This kick is much used by Australian club and international sides and is designed to inflict continuous pressure on the defending team. Having maintained passing and running pressure close to the opponents' line, the attacking team's kicker

will take up position as first receiver at the play the ball. He runs at the defence on receiving the ball and kicks a grubber behind the defensive line into their in-goal area at an angle for his chasing on-side team mates.

Three options are open to the kicking team: to score, to force the defending team to kick the ball or make it dead behind their own dead-ball line, and to tackle their opponents in the in-goal area. The dead-ball and tackle options result in the defending team drop kicking out between the posts from their own try line, allowing the attacking pressure to resume on regaining possession.

THE DROP KICK

Used to restart play from the centre of the 22-metre line and from the try line under the posts, the drop kick can be a match winner in closely fought battles. It is worth one point

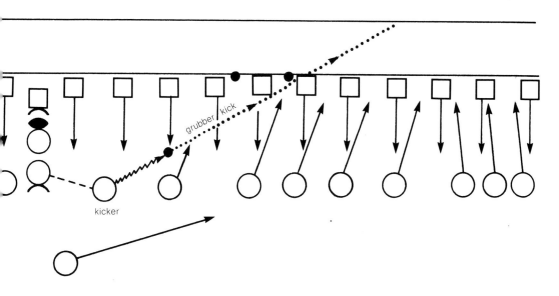

Fig 142   Grubber kick into in-goal area.

when kicked over the cross bar on the full from broken field play, and two points when successful as a penalty kick attempt or to convert a try. Many games are won on a drop kick and having a drop kick specialist in the team is indeed a bonus.

Usually the drop at goal has to be taken quickly as the defending teams will attempt to charge the kick down. A good ploy is to set up a drop goal attempt from the play the ball around 15 metres from the opponents' posts, placing a decoy kicker to call for the pass from the dummy half and the actual kicker on the other side of the ruck. The decoy player attracts the attention of the charging defenders and allows the real kicker, to whom the dummy half passes, extra time to set up his attempt.

THE PLACE KICK

The place kick from the ground is used to start the game in both first and second halves and to restart the game after a score. Its most vital role, though, is to kick at goal after a try or to attempt a penalty kick at goal. It can also be used to kick to touch when awarded a penalty. A good goal kicker is worth his weight in gold and can be a real match winner. Concentration and practice are the essential requirements.

5 Fitness and Nutrition

FITNESS

Introduction

Wouldn't it be nice if someone invented a pill that would ensure instant fitness? There would be no need to spend hours and hours jogging, sprinting, interval running or lifting weights, no need to punish the body by running up hills or on sand dunes, no need to watch the diet, no need to prepare your body carefully for the rigours and bumps, knocks and bruises, no fatigue or suchlike. Well, there is no pill and doubtless never will be. To get the best out of playing Rugby League Football a very high level of fitness must be attained and there is no substitute for hard work. All the diets, drugs and vitamins in the world will never compensate for the hard work required in Rugby League conditioning.

In training, before and during the hard slog of a Rugby League season, the enemies are not ice, snow, rain, sun or wind, but laziness and the easy option. On a wet, cold training night, it is amazing how many players need treatment by the club physiotherapist instead of training. Turning up on time for training requires will-power, self-discipline and the ability to programme oneself into a pre-planned fitness routine. Nothing short of illness should tempt a player away from his routine, which should include training, eating and sleeping patterns.

At the start of the pre-season training programme, rest is particularly important to recoup strength after a hard physical session. So too when strength and endurance improve with training and the team moves on to skills, rest will be needed after skills training to combat mental fatigue. Coaches must be aware of the tell-tale signs of overfatigue in each player — bad temper, frustration, irritability and a decline in concentration — and ease the stress in these players by allowing the crucial recovery time.

No general rule can be laid down for fitness training. Each player is an individual human being with various levels of fitness at any time during the season. His own stresses, either caused through football or at home, are personal to him alone, and no two players will be exactly the same, physically or mentally. The thinking, professionally minded coach or conditioner will construct a personal training programme for each player, allowing for the individual's playing position, his physical condition and his job of work outside the game. The level of fitness improvement will depend on the amount of time and application put into the programme by the player.

Warm-Up and Flexibility

This should be worked on at the start of any training or coaching session to warm cold muscles before moving on to more demanding physical work. The time spent on this exercise would not be as long in warm, comfortable conditions as in cold, wet weather. Muscles and joints throughout the body should be warmed and loosened by a series of light exercises and jogging, gently at first and building to the level of warm-up required by each individual player. Begin with jogging around the field once, the conditioner giving a few stretching exercises when the squad returns to the starting line. Then repeat this, gradually increasing the speed of stretching and working through all the muscles and joints. Move on to running on the spot with high knee-raising, steadily at first, building to sprinting on the spot. Then do some gentle pushing at a wall or solid barrier to stretch the leg muscles, returning to a run round the field with a half-speed sprint over 30 metres or so. Flexibility stretching of the legs, hips, midriff, upper body, arms and neck should be used by the squad once the body muscles are warmed. It may be advantageous to pair off the squad when moving on to flexibility exercises − one of the pair, if required, assisting the other to attain maximum leverage on limbs.

Stamina or Endurance

The vital period for stamina work is in pre-season training. Runs are the best way to build up the endurance level of all players. Cross-country and road running can help build up stamina, but care should be taken when pounding the street as too much road word can cause stress damage to shins or even knees. The correct footwear is essential. Good, sound training shoes should be worn, with a thick cushion of sole to take the impact of foot hitting ground. The distance should be around 8−13 kilometres (5−8 miles) per run with two or three runs per week in pre-season. Topping up the stamina during the season can be done by the occasional long run allied with your club training.

Fartlek running is also advised pre-season. 'Fartlek' is Swedish for speed play, and involves stamina interval running over varied terrain − level stretches, hills, woods, beside streams and through and around generally interesting surrounding. One starts with easy running for about ten minutes, followed by steady speed for about one mile. Then there is a very brisk walk for five minutes, followed by easy running, with about ten 70-metre sprints in between. This is followed by a stop for exercises, and then easy running with sudden acceleration for five or six strides. Full speed sprinting comes next, but up hill for 200 metres. Finally there is fast pace running for one minute. The total distance covered can be 3, 5 or 6 kilometres (2, 3 or 4 miles). The pleasant surroundings play their part in taking the runner's mind off his physical stress.

Similar variations in pace can be achieved on the training ground. Jogging around the field, with increases in speed between the various lines − try line to 22-metre line, half-way line to try line, etc − can assist stamina. Slow interval running is simply a series of sprints over a set distance with walking or jogging over a set time for recovery. This type of training can be practised pre-season, with fast interval running as the season proper approaches.

Table 1 Slow Interval Training (two sessions per week for one month).

Week 1 *1st Session*
Six 100m sprints in 16 seconds with 90-second walk recovery.
2nd Session
Eight 100m sprints in 16 seconds with 90-second walk recovery.

Week 2 *1st Session*
Eight 100m sprints in 16 seconds with 90-second walk recovery.
2nd Session
Ten 100m sprints in 16 seconds with 90-second walk recovery.

Week 3   *1st Session*
Twelve 100m sprints in 16 seconds with 90-second recovery.
2nd Session
Fourteen 200m sprints in 36 seconds with 4-minute walk recovery.

Week 4   *1st Session*
Six 200m sprints in 36 seconds with 4-minute walk recovery.
2nd Session
Two 400m sprints in 80 seconds with 6-minute walk recovery.

Table 2   Fast Interval Training (three sessions for one week).

1st Session

Length of sprint = 40m	Four sprints from jogging start.
	Four sprints from walking start.
	Four sprints from block start.
	Recovery Time: from end of sprint to walking back to start line.
Length of sprint = 60m	Six runs, building up speed over first 30m, sprinting last 30m.
	Recovery Time: as above.

2nd Session

Length of sprint = 60m	Four sprints from jogging start.
	Four sprints from walking start.
	Four sprints from block start.
	Recovery Time: as above.
Length of sprints = 50m, 60m, 70m, 60m, 50m	Recovery Time: as above.

3rd Session

Length of sprint = 80m	Five sprints from jogging start.
	Five sprints from walking start.
	Five sprints from block start.
	Recovery Time: as above.
Length of sprint = 90m	Four sprints, standing start, sprint 30m, decelerate 30m, full sprint last 30m.
	Recovery Time: as above.

Strength

Although it is not required that a footballer pumps iron and becomes a candidate for Mr Universe, it is certainly important to work on a weight-training programme, together with physical exercises, to maintain and build up strength in the legs, arms and upper body. A correct programme can be worked out either by the team conditioner or by the resident weight specialist at the nearest sports and leisure centre.

Weight training will help players' strength greatly, but it can be further increased by various physical exercises at training or by circuit training. Circuit training is simply a series of exercises, against the stopwatch, performed at various exercise stations. As the players become fitter the times taken at each station to complete a set number of exercises should become less. The coach will check each player's time on the first circuit and again at a later session. The distance between stations can vary and this

Exercise			Repetitions	
Sit-ups Light weight held behind head.			20	2
Two-arm curl From below waist to under chin.			10	2
Press behind neck From behind neck to full arm extension.			10	2
Upright rowing From below waist to under chin.			10	2
Half-squat Feet spread to hip width. Lower body steadily with head erect and back straight.			15	2
Press From ground to chest to overhead at arm's length. Lowered by reverse order.			10	2
Bench press Flat on back. Raise to full extension of arms. Lower to chest.			10	2

Fig 143   Suggested weight training programme using multi-gym or free weights.

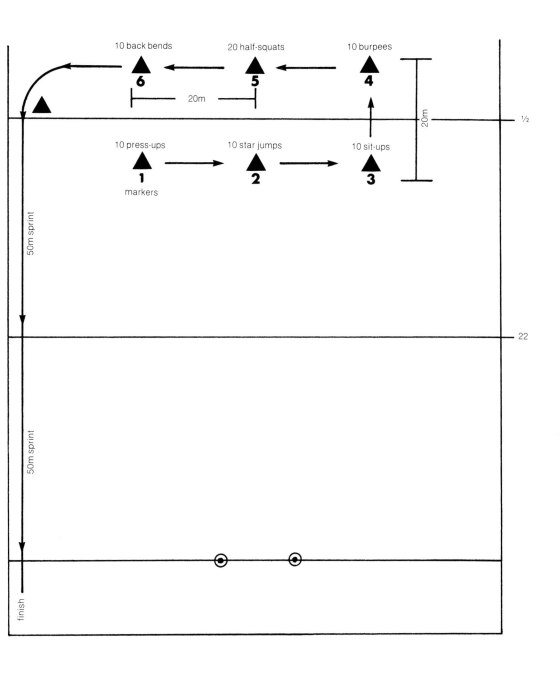

Fig 144   Suggested circuit training set-up using half of field. One circuit shown.

is up to the coach's requirements of fitness levels. The circuit can be concluded with a run and the time of each player is started at the first station and ended as the player crosses the finish line after the run. The correct circuit training will assist fitness in stamina, strength and speed.

Speed

Fast interval running is a good start to speed preparation, then working on grass and, if possible, in spiked running shoes, the players should progress to speed conditioning. This is simply concentrated sprinting over short distances, ending in full 100-metre all-out speed work.

Full speed training begins with knees lifted as high as possible, elbows bent and forearms across the chest, in several 25-metre trots. Speed is not required but the knee lift of each player must be monitored by the coach or conditioner. Next comes three or four 25-metre runs using a natural stride length. This is followed by jog, sprint, jog, at first over regular 25-metre distances and then with variations of jog and sprint lengths. Straight relay races with the team carrying a football are a good exercise to end the sprint training session.

Leg strength is vital to speed. Using bounding exercises in special sprint training exercises gives that extra strength to thighs, knees, calves and ankles. Bounding is stand jumping in forward leaps with feet together. Hopping on alternate legs also helps to build strength. These strength developing exercises should be carefully planned and worked into the sprint programme.

Note: Before any stamina, strength or speed work the player must *always* go through his full warm-up programme.

Recovery

This aspect of fitness training is very important. Giving the correct recovery time period will enable the player to work on his physical training to his full potential. It is impossible for any player to put in quality work if he is in a state of fatigue. The programme of training work to be carried out by the player can include a progressive overload or gradual increase of work or weights, circuit, etc., but time to recover after each discipline must be allowed. Even in skills practice, when most players love to run and handle the football or knock over the bags, the recovery time must be given. As the player becomes fitter the recovery time can be shortened, but this lessening of recovery time must be analysed very carefully by the coach or conditioner to suit each individual player. Be fair in time allowed but demand full effort, with encouragement, when the training programme requires it.

Take care not to allow too long a recovery time between training disciplines because the perspiring player will become cold. Light exercise is recommended to maintain the warmth of the used muscles. Players may even be allowed to replace their tracksuit bottoms or tops during recovery.

NUTRITION

Withstanding the rigours of Rugby League Football requires that the intake and type of food is programmed as clinically as the training. Carbohydrates and fats produce the most fuel for activity. Proteins and minerals provide the repair element for worn-out tissues and supply growth for new. The value of the fuel food is measured in calories, which tell the amount of fuel that a food will produce.

Carbohydrates are the cheapest way to take in calories, and comprise sugar and starches. Sugars include fructose from fruit, lactose from milk, sucrose from cane sugar, and glucose. Starches come mainly from plants. Bread, potatoes, cakes, breakfast cereals, spaghetti, semolina, parsnips, etc. are all starch-based fuel foods.

Fats give twice as many calories, weight for weight, as carbohydrates. Butter, fatty meat, cream, dripping, lard and oils are the obvious fats, but fat occurs also in milk, eggs, nuts, cheese and even lean meat. The danger in eating fats is that they can be digested or absorbed and will give the feeling of 'fullness' for longer.

Proteins are gained through the intake of animal tissue. Meat, fish, milk, cheese and eggs are the most common sources of protein. The most important minerals are calcium and iron. Fish, milk, cheese, eggs, green vegetables and fruit juices all include a good calcium intake. The best source of iron is the animal organs — liver, kidney and heart — but a balance can be obtained from egg yolks, fruit and nuts. Green vegetables too offer an intake of iron.

During pre-season training, usually in warm or hot weather, dehydration can be dangerous, and a good liquid intake before, during and after training is required. Beer is the normal after-training revitaliser, but beware of the misconception of its recuperating power. Beer blocks the release of the anti-diuretic hormone (ADH), which helps regulate the amount of water lost in urine, and so can have a dehydrating effect. Beer can also affect the liver and kidneys, help to destroy the body's vitamin B1 and lose energy.

Good and correct food is a key to good health, and good health is a key to being a good player. Players should check their body weight regularly and correct any increase or decrease by adjusting fuel food intake. Ability in pace, strength and stamina will be governed by the daily diet of correct food. Players should avoid eating a large meal before training, and should practise good eating discipline as they would practise training or football skills. They should not hesitate in seeing their club doctor or GP about health matters. Body and mind are the player's two greatest attributes and should be looked after accordingly.

6 Football Psychology

MENTAL PREPARATION

My dictionary describes psychology as the 'science of the nature, functions and phenomena of the human mind'. The use of sports psychology in Great Britain is not new, indeed for many years now psychology has played an important part in the game build-up in many individual sports such as athletics, tennis, golf, boxing and even chess. In numerous sporting competitions on television we see the participants building themselves up psychologically before the event — the weightlifter, breathing heavily, with a fixed stare and a concentrated mind, the sprint athlete, eyes glazed, loosening and shaking leg and arm muscles, the boxer, eyeballing his opponent while the referee goes through the pre-fight instructions, the tennis player, relaxing beside the umpire's chair, eyes closed and willing himself or herself on. All are preparing themselves mentally, before and during the pre-competition build-up.

The traditional pre-match build-up is no less important in team sports like Rugby League. Some players sit quietly by themselves, muttering and mumbling, some storm around the dressing rooms, shouting unprintable comments. Others, in between long silences, suddenly burst out verbally with comments such as 'Let's knock them down' or 'Come on lads, it's now or never'. Most of us have experienced these things, as a player or coach. But what causes these usually kind, gentle beings to change, so quickly and frighteningly, into almost Jekyll-and-Hyde characters? Tension, nerves

stretched to breaking point, fear, over excitement — all these factors increase as kick-off approaches.

Pre-match mental preparation is as important in Rugby League as practising football skills and fitness, only one small section of football psychology but a vital one to the individual player. Each player will have a slightly differing pre-match mental build-up. Each player must select his best build-up method and work on it. Whoever delivers the pre-match instructions to the team — the coach, the captain, etc. — must take each player's state of mind into consideration during the team talk immediately prior to the game. Shouting and banging the rubbing down table, swearing and threatening the players should they not perform well, should be avoided. Instead, a sensible, normal analysis of the game plan is in order, and, if required, a comprehensive breakdown of the opponents' strengths and weaknesses.

Most experienced players will start preparation early in the week of the game. Some may start by concentrating for ten minutes or more in their leisure time — perhaps before retiring to bed at night — on the journey to the venue. They will see themselves travelling to the game and arriving at the ground. They will prepare, in their mind, visiting the dressing room, walking on to the field and inspecting the ground. They will imagine a crowd already on the terraces, fans calling out to them and wishing them good luck. The thought-preparation must be very positive — no thoughts of losing or bad performance, only of winning and good team and individual involvement.

By midweek the mental preparation transfers to a player's own game. He sets up a routine of thoughts. He sees himself fully involved in the game from the kick-off, pushing himself on, building up a determination to extend his work rate during the coming game. He concentrates on doing the job well, making breaks on attack, defending with tough, hard and fair tackles, kicking well to touch or chipping for himself or team mates, supporting his mates' breaks, and so on. He is determined to play well. He is determined to work hard. He has decided to play a great game and he prepares his mind to do just that. He develops his confidence, and that of his team mates, by his calmness in the dressing room and his sensible and positive approach.

The 1982 Australian touring team was possibly the first to practise serious mental preparation, earning the nickname of 'Invincibles' for their power, pace and skill, but also for their psychological strength. Some old-fashioned thinkers still maintain that the only way to achieve success is with the attitudes and training methods of thirty years ago. To those ostrich-like people I say, for everyone's sake, please use and maintain the learning process. Don't knock it until you've tried it and monitored its results. Players prepare their bodies for a game, let's start preparing their minds.

TEAM AND INDIVIDUAL MOTIVATION

'Motivation' is a word much used in describing team performances. If a team is defeated on the day, questions are often asked like 'Did the coach motivate the team correctly?' 'Were the players motivated?' A captain or coach can help to motivate his team, but the stimulation of a player's interest can only happen if the individual wants it; it stems from the inner self.

One way of increasing motivation is by organising levels of responsibility. Each player responds differently to responsibility — some can handle more than others — but a little care in organising the team can work wonders. Most players also like to be congratulated when they do well, so it is motivating to have the whole team congratulate a player when he scores a try or kicks a goal.

When travelling by team transport to an away game, introduce short, interesting competitions for your team. Show a video on the bus of various competitive sports, grid-iron football, soccer, athletics, etc. But always allow for individual thinking time prior to a game. Give each player his head to complete his mental preparation. In the dressing room before the kick-off the coach or captain, or even a respected team member, can have a motivating influence by speaking to each player, building up their confidence quietly and constructively.

Monthly team talks can also help, when all the players are gathered in comfortable conditions, relaxed and settled, and a little humour is encouraged. Each player may be asked to give a breakdown of his recent form, no holds barred. Perhaps discuss how the team in general has performed.

Video sessions showing edited highlights of the last game, with players doing well on attack and defence, can stimulate interest within the whole team. Correction of faults can also be achieved with videos, but great care must be taken not to pinpoint continuously one individual's mistakes in front of the team. Most players love to know how many tackles they made in a game, how many scrums they won or lost. Distributing a basic stats sheet on video analysis night will enable the team to be better informed.

7 Mini-League

INTRODUCTION

As young children these days are becoming more and more sports-minded, it is only common sense to ease them into their chosen sport rather than throwing them in at the deep end immediately. Tremendous strides forward have been taken by our Rugby Union counterparts over the past few years with the introduction of Mini-Rugby, a specially designed form of the 15-a-side code, honed down to develop confidence and skills in the young enthusiast. Cricket too has realised the need to develop its junior players through a less complicated form of that game.

In Rugby League it was traditional for juniors to play the same game as the seniors, and very little time was allowed for the development of the junior. In some cases, a 9-year-old boy would play against players of 15. As the game gradually moved away from the good old, bad old days into modern thinking, age limits were introduced. This gave the juniors a chance to play against opponents in their own age and physical development bracket. Now, after many years, the game has fallen into line with the other major sports and a standardised form of Rugby League for the really young players, called Mini-League, has been introduced. The participants must be under 10 years old and the whole concept is now geared to allowing the young player to develop confidence, enjoyment and skill. Pilot schemes were run in the Bradford, Halifax and Cumbrian districts, and the opinion was that Mini-League was very successful. Feedback information clearl indicated that juniors loved playing this new form of Rugby League with its freedom of running and passing. The kids are the future We must help them to become the players of tomorrow and Mini-League seems to be at least one answer.

RULES OF MINI-LEAGUE

1. The game to be called 'Mini-League'.
2. The game to be played by under-10-year-olds on 1 September of any calendar year.
3. The maximum number of players per team is eight, with as many as four reserves
4. There is no limit to the amount of substitutions, but each child should play at least half a game.
5. The game to be played in quarters of at least seven minutes' duration, but no longer than ten minutes.
6. The breaks between each quarter to be two minutes.
7. Size of the field. Recommended 60 × 40 metres, but the game can be played in any area.
   - (a) *Safety* The goal post should be outside the playing area.
   - (b) *Width* Consideration should be given to the width of the pitch A too narrow area should be avoided.
8. Size of the ball. Recommended size 3 for this age group, but a size 4 is acceptable
9. There is no limit to the number of tackles during which a team may retain possession

he time which elapses between tackles is
alled a 'tackle period'.

If a team fails to make two passes
etween tackles on three consecutive
ccasions, they automatically forfeit
ossession. The slate is cleaned when two
r more passes are made in any tackle
eriod.

0. A try is scored in the normal way. If it is
cored after only one or two passes in a
ingle tackle period, it is worth four points.
lowever, if a try is scored after three or
nore passes in a single tackle period, it is
vorth six points.

1. After each tackle, all defenders
etreat 5 metres, i.e. there are no markers.
he tackled player must restart play by a
orrect play the ball in a backward direction.
)nce he has played the ball he cannot pick it
ip himself.

2. If the acting halfback is tackled in
ossession, it is a hand-over.

3. Kicks are not allowed:

    (a) The team that wins the toss starts
the game with a tap on the centre
spot.

    (b) After a score, the team which has
conceded the try restarts the game
with a tap on the centre spot.

    (c) There are no kicks at goal.

    (d) Any player who kicks the ball in the
field of play is penalised and the
opposition restart play with a tap on
the point the kick took place.

    (e) If there is any infringement in-goal,
the non-offending team restart play
with a tap on the centre of the
10-metre line.

14. The scrum will consist of three players
vho are to be correctly bound as the front
ow. The non-offending side shall have both
he put in and loose head. The hooker must
pe first to strike for the ball, after which the

props may assist. The ball must come from
the rear of the scrum.

15. The forwards must stay bound until
the
ball has emerged from the scrum.

16. The scrum half feeding the scrum
must immediately retire behind his own
hooker. The non-feeding scrum half must
stand directly behind his own hooker.

17. If the scrum half is tackled after
running with the ball, it is a hand-over.

PRINCIPLES OF THE GAME

1. Each team has been reduced in
numbers to ensure that all players are
totally involved in the action.

2. The rules are designed to increase the
enjoyment of all the children who play.

3. Coaches, administrators, parents and
spectators should follow the Code of Ethics.

4. Criticism of the match officials or the
youngsters involved should not be
tolerated.

5. The game has been scaled down to the
children's level in order to help them
understand both the rules and tactics,
therefore encouraging the development of
game awareness and decision making.

6. The emphasis in training should be on
the development of the fundamental, basic
skills of each child.

7. Ensure that the playing area is safe. For
instance, if playing on half of the pitch
ensure that the goal posts are outside the
playing area.

8. Consideration should be given to the
width of the pitch.

9. The rules are designed to encourage
the players:

    (a) To pass the ball along the line.

    (b) To support the ball.

Glossary

Back One of a team's section of three-quarters numbered 1 to 7.

Big hit A strong, hard tackle.

Blind side At a scrummage, the opposite side of the scrum to where the referee is standing; in normal play, the narrowest distance to the touchline from the ball.

Blind-side prop and second-row forward The two positions furthest away from the referee at the scrum.

Bobby A player in a defensive position between the first line of defence and the fullback.

Bomb kick A punt kick designed to hang in the air, over a shortish distance.

Broken field Normal running and passing etc. in play.

Clearing the line Getting the ball away from one's own try line by a kick or running.

Containment zone The area in which a defending team tackles the opposition without the opposition making ground.

Decoy runner A player who feints to take the pass.

Drop-off A receiving player on attack, who changes the direction of the attack by cutting across the back of the passer.

Dummy half (acting halfback) The player who stands directly behind the ball player at the play the ball and receives the rolling ball from the heel.

Grubber kick A kick along the ground, end over end, with control.

Guts of the ruck The area very close to the play the ball.

Hand-Over When the team which is tackled six times consecutively without the defensive side touching the ball hands over to the opposition to restart play.

Heeling the ball Bringing the ball back into play, after a tackle, at the play the ball.

Hitting the pass Running hard on to a good pass.

Hitting with a pass Finding the receiver with a good pass.

Marker The defending player who stands directly in front of the ball player at the play the ball.

Off-Loading Passing the ball.

Open side At a scrummage, the side where the referee is standing; in normal play, the widest distance to the touchline from the ball.

Open-side prop and second-row forward The two positions nearest the referee at the scrum.

Overlap Creating an outside break, e.g. for a wingman, down the touchline.

Overload Placing more attackers in one area than there are defenders.

Pouring down Letting the ball fall in control from the hands.

Pivot First receiver of the pass from a play the ball.

Ruck The play the ball.

Taking the ball up Running hard, in possession of the ball, against the opposing defence.

Tap kick The ball is placed on ground, touched with the foot and picked up again (hands must be removed from the ball during the kick).

Sweeper *See* Bobby.

Umbrella defence Defensive system shaped like the open canopy of an umbrella.

Index

Acting 'bobby'   100
Acting halfback   12
Attack   76−91
   attacking wide   78−9
   blind side   90
   centrefield   77
   clearing the goal line   77
   close to the ruck   82, 85
   driving forward   78, 91
   gaining possession from kick-off   77
   hand-over   89
   kick-off positions   76
   kick through   88
   open side   90−1
   opposition   88−9
   own team   88
   play the ball   79−85
   scrum   85−8
   tap kick   89−91
   touchline   77

Blind side   44, 90, 91
   prop   2, 43, 101
   second row   6, 43−5, 100, 101
Bobby   97, 99, 100, 106
Bomb   63
   close-in and midfield   106

Captain   4
Catching a high ball   74
   practice   75
Coach   4−6

Defence   93−103
   containment from long kick-off   93−4
   hand-over   101
   kick-off positions   93
   kick through   100−1
   ruck area   97, 99
   short kick-off   94−5
   shuffle defence   97
   six tackles   100
   tap kick   101−2
   umbrella defence   97, 98
   weather conditions   100−1

Discipline   6
Dummy   39
Dummy half   12, 78, 82, 83, 96

Equipment   7
Evasive tactics   36−42
   change of pace   39
   dummy   39
   hand-off   36−7, 39
   hit and spin   39
   side step   37, 39
   swerve   39

Fitness   109−15
   introduction   109
   speed and recovery   114
   stamina and endurance   110
   strength   111, 114
   warm-up and flexibility   109
Football psychology   116−17
   mental preparation   116
   team and individual motivation   117
Fullback   1, 82, 85, 88−9, 91, 96, 97, 99, 100, 101, 106

Game awareness   2
Grids   7

Handling   8−9
   target area   8−9, 11
Hand-off   36−7, 39
Hand-over   89, 101
Hooker   1, 43−4, 94

Kicking game   104−8
   chip punt   106−7
   clearing down-town   104−6
   close-in and midfield bomb   106
   drop kick   107−8
   face kick   107
   grubber kick   107
   introduction   104
   kick through defence   106
   place kick   108

Index

Kicking practices   71–4
  kick and catch   72
  marks and gains   72
  punting between the posts   72
  punting on the point   72
Kicking skills   61–71
  bomb   63
  chip over   63–4, 88, 106–7
  drop kick   67–8
  grubber kick   64, 67, 88
  orthodox punt   61, 63
  place kick   68–71
  spiral punt   64
  torpedo punt   64
  up-and-under   63
Kick-off positions   76, 93

Left centre   1, 85–6, 89, 100
Left winger   1, 37, 82, 86, 88, 89, 93, 95, 100, 104, 107
Lock or loose forward   2, 43–5, 91, 93, 95, 99–100, 101

Mini-League   118–19

National Coaching Scheme   6
Nutrition   114

Open side   44
  prop   1, 43, 94, 101
  second row   2, 43, 44, 45, 93, 95, 100, 102
Opposed practice   103

Passing   8–20
  broken field   11
  circle   18
  count the pass   18
  double file   19
  double run around   17, 81, 82
  drop-off   13, 80
  dummy half   12
  face pass   17
  from ground   12
  miss a man   17
  passing under pressure   12
  practices   18–20
  run around   16, 81, 82
  target area   8–11
  Union Jack   19–20

Play the ball   20, 97
  attacking from   79–85
  defence from   95–9
  one-line defence   95–6
  pass away from   26
  practices   20–6
  relay   25
  set up   21

Regaining possession   32, 34
  dropping on ball   36
  rolling ball   34, 36
  still ball   34
Right centre   1, 85, 86, 89, 100, 107
Right winger   1, 37, 82, 86, 88, 89, 93, 99, 104, 107
Rugby pitch   3
Running with the ball   27–9
  practices   27–9, 34

Scrum half   1, 44, 63, 85–6, 93, 99–100
Scrummaging   42–5, 99
  practices   45
Self-discipline   6
Side step   37
Stand-off half   1, 85–6, 100
Substitutes   2
Support play   29, 32, 33
  channel support   32
  grid-iron rugby   32
  practices   32
  supporting the drive   78
Sweeper   97–9, 100, 106

Tackling   45–61
  blockbuster   53, 61
  block or drive   52, 61
  front-on passive   49, 61
  practices   56–61
  rear tackle   49, 60–1
  side tackle   45, 49
  smother tackle   56
Team spirit   2
Team work   2

Unopposed drills   102–3

Warming up   7, 109–10
Weather conditions   100–1